Exploring Cambridgeshire Churches

Exploring Cambridgeshire Churches

Carolyn Wright

illustrated by Anthony Sursham

Paul Watkins

for

Cambridgeshire Historic Chuches Trust

Stamford 1991

Published by

Paul Watkins

18, Adelaide Street, Stamford, Lincolnshire, PE9 2EN.

ISBN *hardback* 1 871615 91 7

ISBN *softback* 1 871615 92 5

Photoset from the discs of Carolyn Wright in Times Roman (text) and Garamond (headings)

Designed by Martin Smith for Paul Watkins (Publishing)

Printed and bound in Great Britain by Woolnough Bookbinding, Irthlingborough

CONTENTS

PREFACE
and Acknowledgements

Happiness is finding a church open; but then if I had not had the opportunity to meet the keyholders, I would have missed meeting some wonderful people. There was always a little extra information about their church which had escaped the church leaflet and even Pevsner's Guide too. It has been a happy experience gathering the information for this book and I hope it may encourage others to visit our county churches. You will find something special in each and every one.

It began in 1988 when Pamela Tudor-Craig and Robert Van de Weyer introduced me to the delights of Church Tours and to the other activities of the Cambridgeshire Historic Churches Trust. Then, somewhat to my surprise, I found myself on the roads of Cambridgeshire visiting obscure churches in isolated hamlets, rather grand churches in rather small villages, and getting hopelessly lost looking for a friendly spire in city streets. I soon became quite fascinated with churches in general and our county's churches in particular. My family and friends have had much to put up with since I first set out with Pevsner's excellent but somewhat daunting Guide.

My first thanks go to the Trust which gave me this opportunity to see and learn about these churches; and then to Tony Sursham who so generously gave so much of his time and talents to provide the illustrations.

Then sincere thanks to Simon Cotton who supervised many of my early Cambridgeshire explorations, answered endless questions and read through the ever-growing typescript with red pen in hand.

Lynne Broughton and Robert Walker answered still more questions and Pat Saunders encouraged me through difficult times, especially when the Word Processor was getting the upper hand.

Also a very grateful thank you to the many clergy, church wardens and key-holders, who took the time to tell me about *their* church; the plainest church comes to life when you are shown round by someone who cares.

I am also grateful to Philip Riley for his careful proof-reading, John Smith of the Stamford Museum for his helpful comments and especially to publisher Shaun Tyas for his patience and encouragement.

Thank you to Lucy for those hours spent in the library and to Tom who encouraged me on my way. Last but not least I thank Valerie Gravatt who has taken part in so many of these expeditions and whose friendship never wavered during the endless quest for gargoyles, graffiti and Green Men.

Cambridge. January 1991.

Cambridge, St. Mary Magdalene (leper Chapel)

FOREWORD

by the Revd. Robert Van de Weyer

Chairman, Cambridgeshire Historic Churches Trust

At a glance, all churches seem much the same. Outside you see lots of gothic windows, and a tower and a steeple at one end. And inside lots of pointed arches and pews, with some memorials scattered round the walls.

But look closer, and you'll find every church, even the most humble, has unique treasures. In fact each church is a living building, containing priceless artifacts accumulated over hundreds of years. Some of the treasures may be in dark corners, or high up in the roof. Yet if you explore carefully, you shall find exquisite carvings in stone and wood, some of the finest furniture in the country and enchanting relics of bygone ages.

And each church has its own unique story to tell, embodied in its architecture. With only a little rudimentary knowledge of the history of church building you can be as expert as the experts in working out the evolution of the church. You can tell from the shapes of the arches, and the style of the carvings when each bit was added.

In short, you should visit churches with the eyes of a child, hunting for hidden treasure and uncovering the mysteries of the past. There is no happier way of spending a summer's day than driving or cycling to a part of the countryside, and exploring three or four churches in the vicinity. And, remember, no church is boring - every one has its own special story.

This book is a guide for the amateur church explorer in the county of Cambridgeshire - which now includes the four old counties of Cambridgeshire, Huntingdonshire, the Isle of Ely, and the Soke of Peterborough. It doesn't offer detailed descriptions of each church, which are usually rather hard to digest - and anyway are available in more scholarly guides. Rather it points you to the special treasures and features of each church - and so it shows why each church is worth visiting.

It is written by an "amateur" in the proper sense of that word: someone who has got to know the county's churches because she loves them. And it is illustrated by a retired architect who over the years has advised on the care of many of these buildings. Both writer and illustrator are simply inviting you to share their child-like pleasure.

Of course, above all things, churches are places of worship. Today - as in past ages - there are many people who cannot accept every aspect of the Christian creed. But all people, whatever their personal faith, can respond to places of beauty which point beyond themselves to an eternal spiritual beauty. The ancient churches of Cambridgeshire are such places.

Robert Van de Weyer,

Leighton Bromswold. January, 1991.

The Cambridgeshire Historic Churches Trust

The Trust was formed in 1983 to give financial help for the repair of church fabric and to encourage interest in the county's churches.

Cambridgeshire has over 300 excellent churches, many in villages whose population is now so small that they cannot afford to maintain them. The Trust raises money throughout the county, to assist churches in need. It also organises tours of churches and conferences on church architecture. The Trust is a registered charity, and non-denominational.

Please join! Write for information to Robert Walker, 14 Clay Street, Histon, Cambridge. CB4 4EY.

GAZETTEER: CATHEDRALS

ELY CATHEDRAL [F5]

The amazing skyline of Ely Cathedral is visible for miles across the flat fenland, standing on the highest and largest of the old fenland islands. This was the site chosen by Etheldreda to found her monastery in 673, in memory of her father King Anna of East Anglia who was killed by the Mercians. The cathedral is a monument to this event and is one of the most remarkable buildings in Europe. Not only does it contain outstanding work in all the main medieval styles, except Perpendicular, it also manages to combine them in a wholly unique way, to make Ely a dynamic and exciting experience. Viewed from the E by the River Ouse, the building rises in tiers from the Early English E end, via the wide, squat octagon with its beautiful lantern, to a crescendo at the W end. Few buildings can match this complexity and refinement.

The earliest visible building work began with the Normans and exists in the transepts. Following its new status as a cathedral in 1109, the building was extended westwards to the monumental W front. This is what first greets the visitor on arrival and it is an awesome and unusual experience. Instead of twin W towers there is a huge central tower, now topped with a 14th century octagon, and a magnificent SW transept - its N partner fell down in the 15th century and was never rebuilt. This transept has tiers of Romanesque arcading gradually evolving into Gothic as it goes up. The polygonal turrets to the S are absolutely stunning and like nothing else in the country now that the similar W front at Bury St Edmunds no longer survives.

Entering the cathedral through the elegant 13th century Galilee Porch, with its tiers of blind arcading, one enters into the immense cavern of the three storey Norman nave, which marches relentlessly up to the crossing Octagon. It is powerful and stark, and devoid of any ornament, except for the wonderful timber ceiling which was painted by Gambier Parry in 1878. This takes its inspiration from Peterborough, and both cathedral naves create a similar impression, but Peterborough is more ornate and ends in a superb 12th century apsed chancel. There are two doorways in the south aisle which are reminders of the original monastic function of the building. Of these the Prior's Door is the most important and contains some of the best Romanesque carving in the country (also worth seeing is the marble monument to a bishop of c.1150). Go to the E end to view the cathedral's next stage of development. The majestic Early English retro-choir was added under Bishop Northwold, and was copied from Lincoln, with a splendid E wall full of lancet windows.

Then on 22 February 1322, the Norman crossing tower collapsed into the choir. This disaster was transformed into a triumph by the inspiration of John Crauden, prior, and Alan Walsingham, sacrist. They devised what was to be the most innovative and daring architectural feat of the Middle Ages; they rebuilt the crossing in the form of an octagon and then in a moment of architectural virtuosity, they extended it up to a timber lantern resting on eight huge oak supports. These were covered

After the Lady Chapel was finished in the 1350's, there were no more major building programmes. The only Perpendicular work is the elaborate and rather excessive chapel to Bishop Alcock of *c*.1488 and the later 16th century chapel to Bishop West, with Renaissance detailing and sculpture. The cathedral was restored by Sir George Gilbert Scott who put in the choir screen, altered the stalls and reconstructed the lantern of the Octagon. The best fittings are still the Decorated stalls, which originally stood in the Octagon and are embellished with 47 misericords. Ely has the best collection of monuments in the county, including two 13th century Purbeck marble slabs to Bishops Northwold and Kilkenny, the Decorated monument to Bishop Hotham and the unusual memorial to two men who died in a railway accident in 1845.

PETERBOROUGH CATHEDRAL [B3]

At the same time as Etheldreda was establishing her monastery at Ely, thirty five miles north west across the fens, Peada, King of Mercia, was also founding a monastery. This grew to be one of

inside by a complex skin of ribs and stars out of which the lantern explodes. It was a technical and artistic masterpiece and the sense of architectural space is breathtaking. Also of this date is the choir, which also had to be rebuilt, and the equally revolutionary Lady Chapel. The span of the chapel is remarkable and the rich Decorated carving of the canopies undulates in a wave around the room. This and the sumptuous Prior Crauden's Chapel were to be highly influential on Cambridgeshire churches.

the great Benedictine monasteries of Britain, with a famed collection of relics, housed in a magnificent Romanesque building. Whilst Ely, visible on a clear day from Peterborough, gained cathedral status early on, it was only after the Reformation that Peterborough was raised to cathedral rank. Although it has none of the later medieval architectural virtuosity of Ely, it is important because of the almost complete survival of the Romanesque building. The only major alteration has been the addition of the distinctive and idiosyncratic W front which dominates the market square. In the same way as Ely was an administrative centre, so also was Peterborough, and it controlled its own affairs in its Soke in the NE corner of Northamptonshire.

The present building was begun after a fire in the early 12th century, and as with all Norman churches, work started at the E end and developed through to the W. On entering at the W one is presented with an exceptional vista; the strong, robust three storey Norman nave leads without interruption into the Norman chancel finishing in the spectacular apsed E end. This unity allows one to gain an excellent impression of a complete Norman building constructed in about sixty years without stylistic change. There is more decoration than at Ely: zigzag mouldings, decorated tympani, interlacing blind arcading and early rib vaulting in the aisles. The transepts are also Norman and are aisled to the E, containing little chapels, and at the W two smaller transepts were built.

The exterior, though, is less intact, for the tall Norman crossing tower was replaced in the early 14th century by a squat tower (rebuilt in 1882-6 by J. L. Pearson) originally topped by a timber octagon as at Ely, and most of the windows are later medieval replacements. The W front is the main alteration and was added to the Norman nave in the early years of the 13th century. It is entirely in the Early English Gothic style, but is an unusual interpretation of it. It seems the original intention was to have two W towers with a front containing three portals, as at Lincoln, with the central portal being the largest. The whole front was to be one bay deep. After the N tower was built, which has tall blind arcading, it appears the architect changed his mind. The front was extended out further than the transepts to allow for two flanking pinnacled turrets and the two outer portals or niches were made larger than the central one. This means they bear no relation to the W wall behind and the side portals are off centre. The whole thing is topped with pinnacles and gables. Pevsner is very dismissive of this design, but it has an unusual beauty and a monumental grandeur that is like nothing else in the country.

Right in the centre of all this Early English grandeur is a modest two-storey Perpendicular porch built in the late 14th century and now housing the treasury. Also of the Perpendicular period is the bold panelled chancel ceiling, enhanced by a multitude of bosses, which leads us up to the highlight of the later medieval work - the surprising and extravagant retrochoir which surrounds the great Norman apse on the ground floor. It was erected by Abbot Robert Kirkdon between *c.*1496 and 1508 and is similar in detail and quality to King's College Chapel in Cambridge, with its open work parapet and luscious fan vaulting. It has been suggested that John Wastell, who built the fan-vault at King's from 1508, was the designer.

In the retrochoir is the county's most important piece of Anglo-Saxon sculpture, the 8th century Hedda stone. It has standing figures of the apostles set in arcading with a pitched roof above. In the S chancel aisle are the remains of four monuments to Abbots, all carved in Alwalton marble and dating from the early 13th century. The imposing baldacchino over the high altar is of 1894 and probably by J. L. Pearson, who rebuilt the tower. In the S transept S wall is a very early and very fine William Morris window of 1862.

GAZETTEER: PARISH CHURCHES

ABBOTSLEY *St. Margaret* [C7]
A church quite frequently has pinnacles embellishing the tower but here there are four large kingly figures - William the Conqueror, Harold, Macbeth and Malcolm. The link with Scotland goes back to the early 12th century when King David I of Scotland, also Earl of Huntingdon, gave the manor here to Gervase Ridel. It would be good to think one of them was King David, but you must go to the fine church at Conington near the A1 to find a memorial to him. The chancel arch is perhaps all that remains of the earliest 13th century building; the arcades and aisles are from the Decorated period, as is the lovely, though damaged, tomb recess in the S aisle. Major restoration by Butterfield in 1861 and most of the stained glass from this period too. Outside, to the SW, stands the large table tomb of a generous parishioner (d.1688) who left £5 a year to the village, "for ever". The nave and tower are now in the care of the Redundant Churches Fund but the chancel is looked after by the parish and is used regularly for services.

ABBOTS RIPTON *St. Andrew* [C5]
Land for the first church was granted to the Abbot of Ramsey c.974. What you see now is much later - mainly in the Perpendicular style of the 15th century. But look at the S doorway: it has the pointed arch of the Early English period and the S arcade is of the same era. Large Jacobean figures dominate the chancel roof and the altar is late 16th or early 17th century. A tablet (1775) remembers a Sergeant of Arms at the House of Commons. 19th century stained glass and handsome Victorian pulpit.

ABINGTON PIGOTTS *St. Michael* [D8]
A tree-lined path leads to this mainly 15th century church, situated away from the village. A Mass Dial on S buttress and battlements on nave and tower. Tall Perpendicular windows make for a light interior. Two odd little niches either side of tower

arch. Good 17th and 18th century monuments to the Pigott family. A two-decker pulpit remains in fragile condition; a clerk once sat at the lower desk leading the responses. In the chancel floor a large brass, 1460, shows a plainly dressed gentleman with 16 of his children - his poor wife is not to be seen. Look up and see the medieval angels clinging to the nave roof.

Alconbury

ALCONBURY *St. Peter and St. Paul* [B5]
If you enjoy the elegant simplicity of the Early English period, then you must visit this church, and later perhaps go on to Etton in the north of the county. The chancel, arcades, clerestory and tower, with typical broach spire, were built between 1200 and 1290. The chancel gives the greatest delight with blind arcading outlining the lancet windows. However, it is not all Early English, there is one Perpendicular and one Decorated window to the E of the porch. The 15th century roof is supported by eight large angels - no two alike. This is a very lovely place.

ALWALTON *St. Andrew* [B3]

An Early English church with large transepts. Particularly handsome tower; notice the lancet windows and blank arcading on the upper stage; the decorative corbel frieze terminates in battlements, which are also continued on the N stair-turrret. Interesting windows, a double low-side to the S and outside you can see a blocked N low-side. The S aisle was added in 13th century but the late 12th century Norman doorway was retained. Notice also the difference between the C12 N aisle, where four arches were needed, and the finer piers in the three-arched S arcade, built perhaps 100 years later.

ARRINGTON *St. Nicholas* [D7]

Quite a simple country church now, but it was much more imposing in the 13th century, with substantial aisles on both sides of the nave - you can still see the blocked arches in the nave walls. There is a lovely piscina in Jesus College which was copied by several churches in the county, and here is one of them: its size and extravagance well suited to that early building. The simple font is from the earlier Norman church. The tower was partly rebuilt with brick after the Reformation, perhaps at the same time as the aisles were taken down.

ASHLEY-CUM-SILVERLEY *St. Mary* [H6]

Neo-Norman, built in 1845 by the Marquis of Bute whose wife had been patron of the living here. First dedicated to the Holy Trinity, but in 1873 transepts and chancel were added and the church re-dedicated to St. Mary. The previous church of St. Mary, nearby on the Dalham Road, had already fallen into disrepair by 1800 and now only a few gravestones remain. Silverley had its own church too, but all that remains now is the ruined tower which can still be found, hidden away in a dense little wood at the road junction.

BABRAHAM *St. Peter* [F7]

Light and spacious 15th century nave. Splendid lifesize memorial to the Bennet brothers - both baronets who married two sisters. The E window, by Patrick Reyntiens and John Piper, was given in 1966 by Sir Robert Adeane in memory of his father; many other memorials to the Adeane family. A tablet near the S door remembers John Hullier "who burnt at Cambridge during the Marian persecution for his adherence to the Reformed Faith, 1556". A fine pulpit on wineglass stem faces the two-tiered desks for Reader and Clerk. The organ and loft at W end are a 20th century addition and the ghost of an organist's widow is said to visit on occasion.

BAINTON *St. Mary* [A2]

Fine 13th century tower and on its eastern face you can see the outline of the earlier, steeper nave roof. Windows either side of the porch, and the S doorway are Decorated. Our forebears were also interested in recycling materials as is shown by the rather haphazard arch over the outer porch door. During a 15th century rebuilding stones from an earlier, more curved archway were reused. Inside, rounded Norman arcades are the earliest part of the church. Two ornate piscinas grace the chancel with the natural leaf decoration of the 13th century. Monument to Robert Henson, 1755, who received "the applause of all... bribes not being able to corrupt, promises seduce, nor threats deter him from doing his duty".

BALSHAM *Holy Trinity* [F7]

A spacious church with much to see. 13th century tower with more buttresses added in C16 making a grand total of nine. Decorated chancel; early Perpendicular nave. The font is topped by a dramatic 30ft cover, carved in the 1930s by Canon Burrel. This indefatigable rector and wood-carver, together with the

Balsham

villagers he trained, was responsible for much of the craftsmanship here. Two elaborate brasses to earlier rectors in the chancel. John Sleford, 1401, holder of several offices including Archdeacon of Wells and Keeper of the Wardrobe to Edward III, was responsible for building the nave and also the marvellous chancel stalls, with their highly carved double armrests and equally splendid misericords - make sure you see each and every one. The rood screen may date to Sleford's incumbency, but the loft was probably added later. The other fine brass is of John Blodwell, 1462. A modern curiosity is the huge shell case used as a counter-weight for the font cover!

BARHAM *St. Giles* [B5]
A tranquil churchyard surrounds this ancient little building, topped with a sprightly 19th century bellcote. S doorway with zigzag decoration and slightly pointed arch may be late 12th century - the Transitional period between the Norman and Early English styles. Lancet windows with Y-tracery, a sure sign of an Early English building. The bell in the N aisle once hung in the church of St. Mary's in Woolley (demolished in 1961). The bell was given to St. Mary's by the Revd. Mikepher Alphery, a descendant of the Russian Czars, who was given the living here in 1618. He was deprived of the living during the Civil War, but returned after the Restoration and remained here until he retired. He died in 1668. His wife's grave, 1655, is in the churchyard.

BARNACK *St. John the Baptist* [A2]
It really is "one of the most rewarding churches in the county" (Pevsner). Magnificent early 11th century tower with all the details of the Saxon period: long-and-short work in the quoins, triangular windows and decorative pilaster strips of stone, which the Saxon masons loved to use. The massive tower arch dominates the nave. The late 12th century N arcade has wonderful crocketed capitals; in the N aisle also is the quite beautiful late Saxon sculpture of Christ in Majesty. A 15th century work of art - a carving of the Annunciation - can be found in the Lady Chapel. Magnificent early 13th century font - all superlatives here. In the chancel, admire the unusual tracery of the superb E window,

Barnack

c.1325, and the elaborate piscina and sedilia watched over by little medieval faces. A particularly fine memorial to Francis Whitestones is signed by the sculptor, Thomas Greenway of Darby, 1612. Outside, take another look at the Decorated style tracery of the E window. Many good headstones in the large churchyard, some late 17th century, but make sure you see the astonishing fallen palm tree: a memorial to a Gentleman Cadet who died, aged 21, in 1868.

BARRINGTON *All Saints* [D7]
The church overlooks the largest village green in England. The base of the tower is 13th century; but you can see the later building styles and materials as the tower was built. The belfry windows are in the Perpendicular style of the 15th century, the battlements are later still. Admire the handsome 17th century pulpit, complete with sounding board and the massive parish chest. In the S arcade the 15th century wall-painting of "The three

living and the three dead" is still quite vivid; and now look up and admire the marvellous 14th century nave roof. William Dowsing had so much work to do here destroying statues and glass during his Puritan route of destruction, that he noted in his journal that he would need twice the usual payment. In 1871 Edward Conybeare became rector and for the next 27 years did much to restore the church including the restoration of the peal of six bells. Make sure you read his lively instructions to his bellringers displayed in the tower. The metalwork screen was made by village youths taught by Mr. Conybeare. Quite an eccentric - he would ride about the village with his wife perched precariously on the handlebars of his tricycle. Reredos, crucifix and candlesticks by Comper, early twentieth century.

Bartlow

BARTLOW *St. Mary* [F8]

Do visit St. Mary's. There are only two churches with round towers in Cambridgeshire, and here is one; the other is at Snailwell. So first admire the Norman tower then go inside to admire the 15th century wall-paintings. You are greeted by a majestic St. Christopher, carrying the Christ-Child on his shoulder. St. Michael is also here, weighing the souls of the dead; the devil tries to weight the scales but Our Lady uses her influence on behalf of the sinner. On the N wall, the spectacular dragon must be quite relieved that he has finally lost his St. George. The building is mainly early 14th century but has two nice Perpendicular doorways with quatrefoil decoration. The churchyard boasts a splendid 18th century urn and also an art-nouveau metal gravehead, 1908.

BARTON *St. Peter* [E7]

A much smaller building stood here in the 11th century, but nave and chancel were rebuilt c.1300, tower and porch perhaps a century later. The porch, heavily restored, is quite unusual with two large lancets to lighten what may once have been an upstairs room. The many 14th century wall-paintings give us a good idea of how colourful the medieval churches were: over the N door St. Michael weighs the souls of the dead, watched by a devil and also by the Virgin Mary who weights a scale with her rosary. There is St. Christopher, St. John the Baptist and little birds watching over St.Francis of Assisi. Two more birds can be found in the central opening of the Rood Screen, which carries the arms of Thomas Arundel, Bishop of Ely 1374-88. The grand Jacobean pulpit, dated 1635, contrasts with the simplicity of the Norman font. The tower is one of five in the area, all possibly designed by the same mason and built during a forty year period, about 1400. The external limewashed rendering is a 20th century attempt to recreate a medieval exterior, in this case to protect the wall-paintings.

BASSINGBOURN *St. Peter and St. Paul* [D8]

The handsome Early English tower owes much to a major renovation by the Victorians. Attractive timber medieval porch opens on to the light and spacious 14th century interior. The chancel is a beautiful example of the Decorated period. The ogee arch is introduced everywhere: above the doorways, sedilia and really lovely triple piscina. Forty years ago the medieval rood screen was repainted, some said too brightly, but the church seems happy to accept it now. There are small windows to N and

S of the chancel arch, no doubt to throw more light on the rood group; their quatrefoil shape is most unusual. No expense was spared in the 14th century building, even the bases of the octagonal piers have fluted decoration. Poignant seventeenth century marble effigy in chancel floor. Outside, on the chancel N wall, a piscina and door remain from another chapel; and everywhere gargoyles: over windows, doors, under the turret of the outside roodstair and guarding drainpipes. In 1497 money was needed for a new tenor bell, so ten church-ales were held here during the year, no doubt the equivalent of our church fetes today.

BLUNTISHAM-CUM-EARITH *St. Mary* [D5]

The 14th century Decorated chancel is a very uncommon shape for the period: instead of being rectangular, the eastern wall forms a polygonal apse. The nave and aisles are Perpendicular but all was much restored by the Victorians. Under the tower you can see part of the medieval rood screen, with the painted figures of St. George and St. John the Baptist. Lovely font with leafy carving including the ubiquitous Green Man whose face was often used by medieval masons and by painters of pub signs today.

Bottisham

BOTTISHAM *Holy Trinity* [F6]

A wonderful place. Enter through the W porch or Galilee, perhaps the parish church version of the elaborate Galilee at Ely cathedral. The effect of light and space is enhanced by the tall 15th century stone chancel screen, making this a spectacular interior. All largely completed much earlier, between 1300 and 1320, the Decorated period. Many memorials to the Jenyns family, including the romantic Sir Roger holding the hand of Dame Elizabeth, she of the "unblemished reputation". In her memory he endowed the schooling of 20 poor children and the sculpture on the wall of the S aisle commemorates this. More fine memorials behind the parclose screen in the N aisle; here you can also see a

Falconer

unique fragment of a 15th century effigy of a falconer, showing clearly his glove and the bird's tail feathers - who was he and why was he remembered in this way?

BOURN *St. Helen and St. Mary* [D7]

A crooked lead spire tops a very fine 13th century tower with graceful arcading round the belfry. The earliest part of the original church is the fine late 12th century arcade. Notice the extra window added to the clerestory in the 15th century to shed extra light on the rood screen, as at nearby Litlington. Marvellous carving on the medieval pews: notice the Bourn Hall pew near the screen. A window in the N transept shows an Annunciation scene signed by Ninian Comper (1947) with his "strawberry plant" symbol. Reredos and E window are also by Comper. The vestry table, with fine marquetry work, is a former sounding board from the pulpit.

BOXWORTH *St. Peter* [D6]

Particularly attractive view of this neat embattled church if you approach from School Lane. A storm in 1636 necessitated major rebuilding, particularly of the chancel, though the 14th century chancel arch was retained. Records tell of a medieval altar dedicated to St. Katherine. William Cole visited in 1745 and wrote "This is a tolerable handsome church with... a lofty and heavy stone spire." The spire is now no more. Another restoration was necessary in the 19th century and the battlements were added at this time. All the windows, except the E, are by Kempe, resulting in a rather dark interior, but the rather strange windows in the S aisle roof lighten up the interior of this lovingly cared for village church. The stately pulpit, 1682, stands high on its wineglass stem. In the churchyard a large Cheviot rock near the S porch makes an unusual memorial.

BRAMPTON *St. Mary Magdalene* [C5]
Very handsome building with many splendid gargoyles and the interior is just as rewarding. Rebuilt in the 14th century replacing an earlier Norman church. Church building generally slowed dramatically after the Reformation, but this tower was rebuilt in 1635 and is a particularly fine example of the period. Several members of Samuel Pepys' family were buried here though only the tombstone of his sister remains, now in the wall of the S aisle. Three 13th century stalls have exceptional misericords, especially the harvesting scene. The Lady Chapel was made by local craftsmen in 1920, and will be of interest to anyone with an interest in heraldry. You are watched everywhere by quizzical faces in the roof.

BRINGTON *All Saints* [A5]
A secluded church with an early 14th century tower similar to others in this area of Huntingdonshire; notice the quatrefoil frieze just below the spire. The window to the W of the porch is a lovely example of the flowing Decorated style; the window to the E of the porch is a more severe design of the same period. Much restoration of the large chancel was necessary during the 19th century but the double aumbry and the squint beside the arch remain from the earlier medieval building. There is a memorial to members of the United States 303 Bombardment Group who were stationed at nearby Molesworth.

BRINKLEY *St. Mary* [G7]
A little owl sits on one of the gateposts outside this little flint church with its unusual brick medieval porch. Flint flushwork frieze around base of tower. The chancel was rebuilt in 1874 but the E window remains from an earlier building, *c.*1300. 17th century pulpit. Poignant memorial near the font to two infants: a girl who lived for four months and a boy who died whilst being christened when only four days old.

BROUGHTON *All Saints* [C5]
The newly-restored 15th century wall-paintings are quite lovely. The Day of Judgement, or Doom, above the chancel arch, must have been a sobering message for any nervous villagers. On the left, naked figures rise from their tombs on Judgement Day and to the right the damned are being driven into Hell; one unfortunate soul is suspended over a cauldron. On the S arcade Adam and Eve are expelled from the Garden of Eden. The nave roof holds carved angels with musical instruments. Most of the building periods are here: the Norman font, the Early English chancel, the Decorated arcades, the tower and most of the building are Perpendicular and the Communion Rail is 18th century.

BUCKDEN *St. Mary* [B6]
This lovely church stands out against the red brick of the Palace, which belonged to the Bishops of Lincoln when that diocese stretched from the Humber to the Thames. The two-storeyed S porch dates from the late 1400s and no expense was spared in its decoration, especially its S face. It has a curious frieze of animals over the doorway, more little faces above and even on the weathered pinnacles. Even the battlements above the doorway are decorated too. The vaulted porch roof has a central boss of the Virgin Mary. The interior 'framing' over the small porch windows is similar, though on a grander scale, to that at Easton and Buckworth. The Perpendicular windows of the main body of the church are spectacular from the outside and, with their clear glass, wonderfully lighten the interior; and there is much to admire. It is almost all mid-15th century, but the medieval masons retained the Early English sedilia, piscina and the two priests'

doorways in the chancel. Jacobean pulpit and lovely 16th century Passion scenes in the panels of the Readers' desks. Now look up; everywhere there is something to see and admire: angels in nave and chancel, strange grotesques and others in the S arcade. Laurence Sterne (1713-1768), author of *Tristram Shandy* and publisher of many volumes of sermons, was ordained here in 1736.

BUCKWORTH *All Saints* [B5]

Lovely in its isolation - you are unlikely to happen upon it by chance - but do seek it out. It has a particularly lovely 13th century steeple, best seen when approaching from Leighton

Bromswold when the three tiers of lucarnes give a delicate, almost fragile look to the spire. Notice the Early English details on the W wall of the tower, especially the rose window and Y-tracery of the bell-openings; also admire the sweeping view which the gargoyles have long enjoyed. The large porch has a stringcourse, stone seats and arcades 'framing' the windows similar to those at Easton. Restoration has been carried out recently and the brightly

Buckworth

painted bosses in the roofs catch the eye. In the N aisle, read the memorials to villagers who died as far apart as Ladysmith and the Vimy Ridge. A small congregation takes great pride in its large church.

BURROUGH GREEN *St. Augustine* [G7]

This large flint church is a complicated sort of building, so do walk all the way around: surprising gables and large windows of the seventeenth century, and other earlier blocked windows and doorways. You can see where chapels once stood against the N and S walls, perhaps built in the 14th century when the tower was

in the course of construction. The chancel is earlier: the decoration of the sedilia and double piscina, as well as the lovely east window, are about 1300. The pulpit looks Jacobean but in fact is work of Victorian craftsmen. Effigies of the de Burgh and Ingoldesthorpe families, who were Lords of the Manor here.

Burwell

BURWELL *St. Mary* [F6]

Majestic, magnificent - this "most perfect example in the county of the Perpendicular ideal of the glasshouse" (Pevsner). Wonderful feeling of light and space in this spectacular 15th century building, probably designed by Reginald Ely, the first master mason of King's College Chapel. Remarkable nave roof, 1464, with a whole host of animals, angels, dragons and more. In the chancel still more wonderful figures and faces in oak and stone. It has been much restored but admire the elaborate niches with some of the original paintwork. A remarkable brass in the chancel floor shows the last Abbot of Ramsey who was well rewarded with a generous pension when surrendering his abbey. The brass, made in his lifetime, portrayed him in richly decorated vestments; later it seems he thought it more prudent to have the brass reversed and the new portrait shows him as a simply dressed cleric. You must look at the tower for evidence of the earlier building, there is a blocked Norman window and also a blocked bell-opening.

BURY *Holy Cross* [C4]
The tall lancet windows of the 13th century tower are lovely examples of the Early English style. A century later another porch or chapel stood here and remains of it can still be seen. The 12th century chancel arch with strong Norman carving and the large primitive font both remain from an earlier building. Most medieval churches had one low-side window, usually to the S of the chancel; here there are two, and both retain their wooden shutters. The small 14th century lectern is still in use today; it is a lovely delicate piece of craftsmanship and stands on a 13th century stone base. Dedications to the Holy Cross are usually found with churches of Saxon origin. 16th century wills refer to the churchyard of Our Lady at Bury; the dedication may have changed at the Reformation, or perhaps the now demolished chapel or an altar was dedicated to St. Mary.

BYTHORN *St. Lawrence* [A5]
Contrast the steep pitch of the earlier chancel roof with the flat nave roof, which became fashionable in the late Middle Ages. On the W wall of the tower is an unusual triangular shaped window of the Decorated period. The 14th century spire was declared unsafe after the last war and the villagers now have to live with a

very strange looking affair. Vibrations caused by the vast numbers of aeroplanes in this area were said to have caused the damage; but some who saw it being pulled down testify that the spire was still quite safe and that it stubbornly resisted each stone being removed. Inside, notice the differing styles of the arcades; in the N the piers are alternating round and octagonal and to the S they are quatrefoil. Both built about 1300, though the N may be a little earlier. In the chancel the piscina is now at ankle level as a result of the Victorian trend of raising the floor for the High Altar. Before you go, walk around outside to see the little whiskered face over the N doorway.

CALDECOTE *St. Michael and All Angels* [B4]
If you are interested in towers then you might like to know that this is thought to be one of five in the area, possibly designed by the same mason; the others are Barton, Coton, Hatley St. George and Knapwell. All were completed during a forty year period about 1400. The outside moulding of the W window is supported by two little faces; one looks just about to sneeze. A simple aisleless church. There is a little Decorated niche by the chancel arch with more medieval faces and traces of original paintwork. Attractive 18th century headstones in the churchyard with cherubs and roses struggling through moss and ivy.

CAMBRIDGE *All Saints* Jesus Lane [E7]
Designed by Bodley in 1864. The growing parish needed a larger building to replace the medieval church of All Saints in Jewry. This stood opposite Trinity gate, where the Saturday craft market is now held. Inside, the stencilled wall decorations and delicately painted roofs are by the William Morris workshop. Superb E window by Morris, Burne-Jones and Ford Madox Brown and many other good examples of 19th century stained glass throughout. The wheatsheaf symbol of Kempe can be seen here, and note also the peacock wings he often gave to his angels; panels on the pulpit are also by Kempe. All Saints is now in the care of the Redundant Churches Fund.

CAMBRIDGE *St. Andrew the Great* St. Andrew's Street [E7]
A very imposing church by Ambrose Poynter, 1842-3, replacing an earlier medieval building. Sadly no longer in use as a parish church. There is a monument here to Captain Cook, his wife and six children. His wife lived to the age of 94 and is buried here with two of her children.

CAMBRIDGE *St. Andrew the Less (The Abbey Church)* Newmarket Road [E7]
This little church was built early in the 13th century for the villagers of Barnwell by the Augustinian canons of Barnwell Priory. It is a lovely Early English building and was once the mother church of a large parish which still bears its name. In the last century it fell into great disrepair and was restored by the Cambridge Antiquarian Society. An elegant rood screen divided nave and chancel until at least 1845 but nothing remains of it now. From outside the E window is a simple triple lancet, but inside is decorated with slender columns of Purbeck marble.

CAMBRIDGE *St. Augustine of Canterbury* Richmond Road [E7]
Built in 1890 as a dual purpose building for school and church. Resembling more a large and friendly home, St.Augustine's is an active community centre as well as a place of worship and is now one of the five churches of the Parish of the Ascension.

CAMBRIDGE *St. Barnabas* Mill Road [E7]
A church which recently had the welcome problem of needing more seating for the growing congregation. The interesting solution was to move the altar to a raised dais at the West end and the benches into a collegiate arrangement. No major structural alterations were necessary to this yellow brick church, built 1869-88. A porch has recently been added at the E end of the chancel and the Victorian wall decoration has been retained.

CAMBRIDGE *St. Benedict (St. Ben't)* St. Benet Street [E7]
Believed to be the oldest church in Cambridgeshire. The tower was built about 1025 and Saxon 'long and short' work can be seen at the quoins, or corners, supporting the massive chancel arch.

Cambridge –
St Bene't

Two lion-like animals support the arch itself. The nave and chancel are typical of a Saxon church, but the pointed arches of the arcade are from the 13th century rebuilding. Nicholas Toftys from nearby Landbeach was responsible for the 'new' roof here in 1450. Many colourful figures in the roof of the N aisle with crowns and shields, and cheerful angels in the nave. A modern masterpiece stands in the N aisle - a bronze crucifixion by Enzo Plazotta.

CAMBRIDGE *St. Botolph* Trumpington Street [E7]
Dedicated to the patron saint of travellers, this church stood by the Trumpington Gate of medieval Cambridge and for a while was chapel to Pembroke College. Mainly 14th century building. Tower, *c.*1400, is topped by figures of the four evangelists. The

splendid font and cover will catch your eye, but also look up and admire the 19th century stencilling on the roof by Bodley. Perhaps not so admirable is the Plaifer monument, 1609, which Pevsner describes frankly as "absurdly bad". Outside there is yet another Cambridge churchyard/garden with summer flowers in profusion which do not quite conceal the interesting headstones.

CAMBRIDGE *Christ Church* Newmarket Road [E7]
The red brick exterior with large pepper-pot towers seems to be a 19th century echo of King's College. The church was built to the design of Ambrose Poynter in *c*.1837. Recently some innovative remodelling took place and the tall interior has been made into two floors. The parish hall now occupies almost the entire ground floor with the church 'upstairs' and so it is still possible to enjoy the brilliant stained glass in the E window. There are handsome central and galleried side pews and the original pulpit and lectern. An inscription on the font cover tells that it was "purchased chiefly by penny subscriptions from 1200 children in 1834."

CAMBRIDGE *St. Clement* Bridge Street [E7]
A 13th century interior remains, but the exterior walls are a result of rebuilding in the early 16th century. Wall-painting on E chancel wall of the Lord in Triumph; St. Clement seen with the Anchor of his martyrdom. Since 1986 the Anglican congregation has shared the church with the Greek Orthodox Parish of St. Athanasios and four large icons now enrich the nave. The tower,1821, replaced a "disgraceful wooden steeple."

CAMBRIDGE *St. Edward King and Martyr* Peas Hill [E7]
This dedication is usually evidence of a pre-conquest church as Edward was declared a martyr in 1001. The lowest stage of the tower may well be Saxon. St. Edward's was rebuilt after the disastrous city fire of 1174. The graceful piers and arcades are from another major rebuilding about 1400; a little later, in 1446, the chancel aisles were added to provide chapels for the colleges of Trinity Hall and Clare. Three martyrs of the Reformation preached from the handsome linenfold pulpit: Latimer, Barnes and

Bilney; they are also remembered in a window in the S aisle. More fine linenfold panelling on the Nightwatchman's chair in the chancel. Close by the medieval 'angel' font in the S aisle is a memorial to Frederick Maurice, the 19th century preacher, writer and social reformer. A tranquil church, with a delightful little churchyard where the headstones are almost lost to view in the summertime amongst roses, flowering shrubs and trees.

CAMBRIDGE *St. George*. Chesterfield Road [E7]
The Chesterton area of Cambridge grew rapidly during the Thirties and in 1932 a small church was built for the expanding community. In 1938 Thomas H. Lyon was commissioned to design this rather grand building. Thirty years previously he had designed a very similar church, also with a tower, in South Australia. Contains several works by the talented sculptor Loughnan Pendred (1902-1980) who lived in nearby Milton.

CAMBRIDGE *St. Giles* Chesterton Lane [E7]
The Saxons built a Minster church here but the Priory moved out to Barnwell. Picot, the first Norman Sheriff of Cambridge, and his wife are said to have built a church here in 1092, as an act of Thanksgiving after his wife had almost died. The chancel arch of this little church remains as the arch between the S aisle and chapel. There is some 'long-and-short' work on the lower part of the jambs, usually a sure indication of a Saxon building. The church was rebuilt in 1875 by Healey of Bradford; the stained glass is all Victorian; the E window is a particularly fine example of Kempe's work.

CAMBRIDGE *Church of the Good Shepherd* Mansel Way [E7]
A large handsome brick church designed in 1954 by S. E. Dykes Bower using the Early English Style throughout, including the font and altar. The S chapel is dedicated to Nicholas Ferrar (1592-1637), founder of the religious community at Little Gidding in Huntingdonshire. The first vicar here was a member of the Oratory of the Good Shepherd, a religious order founded at Little Gidding in 1913.

CAMBRIDGE *Great St. Mary* Senate House Hill [E7]

An outstanding example of the late Perpendicular style, perhaps by John Wastell, the last master mason of King's College Chapel. It is quite similar to the churches at Saffron Walden and Lavenham and the same masons may have been involved. The tower took just over 100 years to complete and was not finished until 1600. The church is a tribute to the local merchants who paid for the building and furnishing; though the oak timbers in the roof were the gift of Henry VIII. Churchwardens' accounts show that the W face of the screen was to be copied from that of Thriplow, and the loft itself to be 8 feet wide; the work was finished *c.*1523. Cranmer, Latimer and Ridley all preached here. The Puritans destroyed all the medieval glass, which was replaced in the latter part of the last century. The galleries were designed by James Gibbs in 1734 for the growing number of students and the ingenious sliding pulpit was installed 100 years later. The quality of the interior emphasizes that this is the University Church.

CAMBRIDGE *Holy Sepulchre (The Round Church)* Bridge Street [E7]

In 1140 local members of the "fraternity of the Holy Sepulchre" asked the Abbot of Ramsey for land on which to build their church. Many of the 11th and 12th century churches were paid for by small local communities in this way, but it is only when records survive, such as those kept at Ramsey, that we have any detailed accounts. Jerusalem had been captured by the Turks 40 years earlier, hence the dedication. The dome roof, part of the Victorian restoration, rises above the massive Norman pillars; the gallery above is also Norman. Medieval ceilings remain in the choir and north aisle. The "candlesnuffer" was added to the tower during the restoration in the 1840s, and the S aisle added at this time. Other round churches which survive are in Northampton, the Temple Church in London, Little Maplestead in Essex and the castle chapel at Ludlow.

CAMBRIDGE *Holy Trinity* Market Street [E7]

A major fire in 1174 destroyed much of the city including an earlier building here. The present church is impressive and the tall 14th century nave adds to the light and space. The transepts were added a century later and the vast clear windows are wonderful examples of the Perpendicular style. Holy Trinity has long been associated with the Evangelical Movement and the memorials on the chancel walls make fascinating reading. Look at the tower arch, supported by flying buttresses when the elegant nave was built, and still larger buttresses to support the later 15th century roof.

CAMBRIDGE *St. James* Wulfstan Way [E7]

Designed by David Roberts and dedicated in 1955; already three additions have been necessary to fulfil the needs of an active parish. The Focus Institute opened here in 1976. It has a pleasant white-washed interior and St. James' proves that a church does not have to be ancient to have a special atmosphere of peace and welcome.

CAMBRIDGE *St. John the Evangelist* Hills Road [E7]

A large red brick church designed in 1896 by Gordon, Lowther and Gunton in the Decorated style much favoured by the Victorians. The E window is particularly fine. Most of the carving throughout the church was done by two local craftsmen who were regular worshippers here. Painting of the Transfiguration by R. Wearing, 1985, in S aisle.

CAMBRIDGE *St. Luke* Victoria Road [E7]

A large church built in 1874 by W. Basset-Smith close to an equally large United Reformed church. In 1988 it was decided to pull down the United Reformed building and modify St. Luke's for the use of both congregations. The first joint service was held on Christmas Eve, 1989. The early 14th century style used by the Victorians remains. Victorians raised the chancel floors to increase the importance of the altar; now the lovely piscina and sedilia hang suspended as decoration only since the floor has been lowered to the level of the nave. The handsome western gallery and the rails in front of the organ came from the United Reformed Church. The apse, transepts and easternmost part of the nave are now used for worship. The western end of the nave now has two floors and all the modern amenities needed by two busy city congregations.

CAMBRIDGE *St. Mark* Barton Road [E7]

A very handsome building both inside and out. Designed by Philip Day in 1901, using the Early English style with lancet windows, blank arcading and a large apsed chancel complemented by a low stone screen. St. Mark's replaced an earlier iron and timber church designed by Richard Rowe of Cambridge (who made no charge for his services) and built in 1871 as a mission church in the parish of Grantchester.

CAMBRIDGE *St. Martin* Suez Road [E7]

A church hall was built here in 1932 but it was not until 1961 that funds were raised to build St. Martin's. The architects were Paterson and Macaulay and the A-frame triangular design is carried throughout the interior. A community centre was completed in 1972 and in 1980 this active parish built a daughter church, St.Thomas, in nearby Ancaster Way.

CAMBRIDGE *St.Mary the Less* Trumpington Street [E7]

Consecrated in 1352 when known as St.-Peter-without-Trumpington-Gate, and the college chapel to Peterhouse until 1632. No chancel arch, no arcades but wonderful Decorated style details throughout. The windows are identical to those in the Lady Chapel at Ely, so perhaps the hand of Alan of Walsingham, Sacrist of the Cathedral, was at work here too. Churchwarden's initials are engraved on the font cover, 1632. George Washington's great-uncle is remembered here, and the Stars and Stripes, together with the eagle, are plain to see. Pulpit with sounding board, 1741. The High Altar is by Sir Ninian Comper (1913) who also designed the Mendel Cross and the lower part of the E window; the remainder of the window is by Kempe. The simple Lady Chapel was added in 1931. Make sure you see the garden here at Little St. Mary's, it is delightful all year round.

CAMBRIDGE *St. Mary Magdalene (Leper Chapel)* Newmarket Road [E7]

It would have been isolated when first built, but still within a reasonable walk of the medieval city. Almost certainly being used as a hospital from about 1150 and not only for lepers. The chancel would have been reserved for the priests and the hospital area, perhaps with straw pallets on the floor, would have been in the nave. The large corbel in a N window looks rather out ofplace, and may well have come from Denny Abbey much later. The simplicity of the interior is enriched by the marvellous decoration of the chancel arch. The round W windows are typical of the period but the larger window was put in by Sir Gilbert Scott during the restoration in 1867. The Chapel has had many uses: as a barn, a cattle shed and for a long time as a storehouse for the Stourbridge Fair, once one of the most important Fairs in Europe.

CAMBRIDGE *St. Matthew* St. Matthew's Street [E7]

Designed by Richard Rowe in 1866 and a very bold interior presents itself. In the shape of a Greek cross, with four equal arms; the spacious central area rises dramatically to the octagon lantern. Rowe had worked at Ely with Gilbert Scott c.1850 and had been responsible for detailed drawings of the octagon. Later, c.1873, when Surveyor to the Dean and Chapter, he supervised the restoration of the octagon. One of the windows is dedicated to his wife Sarah. Only 3 of the original stained glass windows remain behind the altar, two being destroyed when bombs dropped nearby during the last war. Just behind the church the new vicarage is also of innovative design.

CAMBRIDGE *St. Michael* Trinity Street [E7]

Built in the early 14th century by Hervey de Stanton, the founder of Michaelhouse College, to serve both the college and the surrounding parish. The S chapel is in true Decorated style; notice the highly elaborate niches each supported by a worn little angel. The chancel retains the elegant 14th century piscina and sedilia; the 18th century choir stalls are thought to have come from Trinity College. A fire necessitated a major restoration in the last century by Gilbert Scott. In 1966 the church was united with Great St. Mary's and the nave is now used as St. Michael's Hall.

CAMBRIDGE *St. Paul* Hills Road [E7]
A large red brick church designed by Ambrose Poynter in 1841 using the Perpendicular style for the window tracery. The aisles and transepts were a later addition. Attractive E window replaces the one blown out when bombs dropped nearby in World War II.

Cambridge ~ St Peter

CAMBRIDGE *St. Peter* Castle Street [E7]
A small tranquil place, parts of which date to the 11th century. It fell into total disrepair and was rebuilt in 1781 using the original stone. The arch in the N wall is from the original building. Almost devoid of ornament except for the quite remarkable font, with mermen at each corner, which may well have stood in that early church; it is supported by a 14th century base. Now safe in the care of the Redundant Churches Fund, St. Peter's provides quiet welcome for all.

CAMBRIDGE *St. Philip* Mill Road [E7]
The present, Early English style, brick building was built in 1890 by William Wade of St. Neots, at a cost of just under £2,000. It replaced an earlier wooden chapel nearby. Nicely carved pulpit. The western end of the large nave has recently been converted into pleasant parish rooms and offices.

CARLTON *St. Peter* [G7]
No spire here to guide you but medieval bells hang in the double bellcote. The walls are patched with plaster and lean outwards rather alarmingly. The E window has recently been restored following the design of original tracery, but the church cannot have changed too much over the years. The 15th century font has symbols of the Resurrection. There is an early 17th century pulpit and a single tie-beam and kingpost roof. The medieval rood screen has been moved to the W end of the nave. In the chancel a monument recalls a vicar and his wife, and their seven children who all died in infancy.

CASTLE CAMPS *All Saints* [G8]
Attractively located on high ground, half a mile or more from the village. The church once stood within the outer bailey of the castle built in 1068 by Aubrey de Vere, Earl of Oxford, and was probably the garrison chapel. Nothing remains of the original wooden church, nor of the elaborate fortifications which once covered at least eight acres. The 13th century S doorway and piscina are the oldest parts of the present church, though building continued over the next two hundred years. Extensive restoration was necessary around 1850 when tower and porch were rebuilt.

CASTOR *St. Kyneburga* [B3]
This church must have been one of the very finest in the country when it was built in the 12th century; perhaps that is why the actual dedication date in 1124 was carved above the priest's door on the S chancel wall; very few such carved records have survived. Bands of rich arcading surround the magnificent central tower which is topped by a 14th century spire. The interior is splendid too: the decoration on the piers supporting the tower; the

Castor

CATWORTH St. Leonard [A5]

14th century for the most part, the large-windowed clerestory is later. There are faces everywhere, inside and out and a fine Early English S doorway. In the chancel a disfigured piscina dates from the same era; it must once have been double but has been crudely cut. Nicely carved wooden gate, flanked by unusual stone walls. Nave roof and rood screen were restored in 1939. The elaborate chandelier came from Brasenose College, Oxford. An interesting churchyard, with a lovely memorial to a young boy, standing with cricket bat in hand.

CAXTON St. Andrew [D7]

Another church, like Old Weston, that now stands quite apart from the modern village. The chancel was built in the 13th century. The piscina is original, also the strange stone seat which has an 'armrest' with a single small star design similar to that on the stone seat at Houghton. The E window is a memorial to Dr. August John Wright, Surgeon, who died in 1849 and must have been much admired by the donors, who were 430 patients and friends. In the 17th century the church was in such a ruinous state that the roof had fallen, but it was rebuilt and in 1672 two new bells, by Christopher Graye, were hung. Again in the last century the church was only saved by a national appeal and a major restoration took place 1863-9.

wall-paintings, particularly that of St. Catherine; the late medieval roof with painted angels; a small Saxon sculpture in the chancel, not unlike that of St. Peter at Wentworth. St. Kyneburga, a Mercian princess, was the foundress and Abbess of the convent here. She died *c.*680 and her relics were later translated to Peterborough.

CHATTERIS *St. Peter and St. Paul* [D4]

Set back from busy Market Hill. Much restored in 1909 by Blomfield, thanks to the generosity of a sexton's son who made his fortune in the New World. Very little remains of the 14th century church except for the lower part of the W tower and the nave arcades. 20th century faces, as well as more ancient figures, gaze curiously down from the roof. Lovely carving on the pulpit in memory of the vicar's son who fell at Flanders. Stained glass window dedicated to a former choirboy who was posthumously awarded the Victoria Cross.

CHERRY HINTON, Cambridge *St. Andrew* [E7]

A wonderful interior; the height, light and simplicity of this 13th century church must be seen. It is all so elegant - in the chancel lovely triple sedilia and an equally lovely double piscina with dogtooth moulding. Stone faces stare down from the nave roof. Medieval benches remain in the N aisle and above them hangs a sculptured oak panel, formerly the altarpiece in St. Andrew the Great in Cambridge. Monument in chancel by Flaxman, to Walter Serocold (1794), of whom it was said "the king has not a more meritorious captain". Recently a community hall has been added to the N.

CHESTERTON, Cambridge *St. Andrew* [E6]

The Manor of Chesterton originally belonged to the King and in 1217 Henry III presented the church and living to Cardinal Guava, in gratitude for rescuing England from almost certain civil war during the previous reign of King John. The advowson remained with Vercelli Abbey until 1436, when Henry VI finally retrieved it and gave it to Trinity college. There is much to admire here. 15th century benches with carved arm-rests as crouching lions, griffons, dragons and other beasts. The roofs are full of carved faces and angels and there is a spectacular late 15th century Last Judgement above the chancel arch. Lovely piscina and triple sedilia with little faces supporting the vaulting in each one. On the wall of the N aisle, near the porch, read the memorial to the "daughter of the African". Interesting headstones in the large churchyard.

CHESTERTON Nr. Peterborough *St. Michael* [B3]

The handsome Early English tower is easily seen, but to reach the church you must find the 'daisy lane' between the bus stop and post box. The S doorway is also Early English but much of the interesting interior is early 18th century, notably the chancel, many windows and the small baluster font. Fine monument in N aisle to the Belville family, 1611 - the couples facing each other and the children clustered below, kneeling on tasselled cushions.

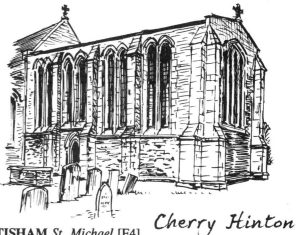

Cherry Hinton

CHETTISHAM *St. Michael* [F4]

A lovely country church, with wooden porch, shingled bell-turret, and a highly polished interior. A brick wall surrounds the churchyard and all is lovingly cared for. A 13th century, Early English, building with no chancel arch. The roof is painted in the style of the Arts and Crafts Movement of the late 19th century, when considerable restoration took place. Fragments of Norman sculpture are kept in the vestry.

CHEVELEY *St. Mary and the Holy Host of Heaven* [G6]

A church dedication unique in the country, although dedications to St. Mary alone are by far the most common. A cruciform building with central tower of the early 1300s. The octagonal top was added a little later and is best seen from the S, away from the stair turret. Walk all around and notice windows of three periods: simple Early English lancets, flowing tracery of the Decorated period and the more formal Perpendicular style. Inside, stand beneath the crossing to see the deep grooves left by the bell ropes on the arches. Angels carrying shields support the chancel roof and there are nicely carved bench ends on some of the choir stalls. Splendid font with shields depicting the Instruments of the Passion and Signs of the Evangelists.

Chippenham

CHIPPENHAM *St. Margaret* [G6]
Land here was given by Richard I to the Knights Hospitallers about 1190 and although most of the church dates from the 13th century, some evidence of the Norman building remains; notably the window in the chancel, now blocked. Medieval graffiti can be found on many of the piers, particularly in the N arcade; some of it is thought to be very early. Mrs. Pritchard in her book *English Medieval Graffiti* suggests that a scratched drawing, which is upside down on the pillar next to the N parclose screen, may be a caricature of Richard I, making it *c.*1190. An Indulgence for rebuilding the church after a fire was granted in 1447 and no doubt much stone was reused at this time. A spectacular wall-painting of St. Christopher on N wall, and remains of colour on piers and arches throughout. At first glance the Rood Screen appears to be decorated with delicate scrolls and leaves, but closer inspection reveals little faces on almost every cusp, and also on the pinnacle-like decorations as well. Similar faces and pinnacles can be seen on the rood screen, now in the N aisle, at St. Andrews, Soham - the same craftsman maybe. Very fine monument in chancel to Thomas Revet (d.1582) with his two wives and four children.

CHRISTCHURCH *Christ Church* [E3]
Large Victorian church designed by John Giles in 1864. Attractive interior with white painted apsed chancel and cheerfully coloured roof. Until this church was built, the area was known as Brimstone Hill as the vicar of Upwell was supposed to have chased the devil away from his village to this spot.

COATES *Holy Trinity* [D3]
Designed in 1840 by J. Wild in the Norman style; the aisles were added later. Unusual in having a NE tower. This is one of the so-called Commissioners' Churches which were built to provide churches for the new urban areas as a result of a Parliamentary Commission of 1818.

COLDHAM *St. Etheldreda* [E2]
A tidy little church built, in the Decorated style, in 1875. The pews slope alarmingly to the outside walls, as do many others on the soft fenland soil, but no doubt it is all safe enough. The Victorians insisted on the elaborate piscina and sedilia, and notice the scenes on the three large tiles in front of the altar.

COLNE *St. Helen* [D5]
Rebuilt by William Fawcett the Cambridge architect, using many materials from the original church which had collapsed in 1896. The low pitched roof is attractively painted. Several memorials from the earlier church remain, including an interesting board dated 1690 showing the generosity of several parishioners with their bequests of loaves of bread and money for the poor. The original church stood a little distance away; only parts of the crumbling porch survive.

COMBERTON *St. Mary the Virgin* [D7]

An interesting church and churchyard. Inside, the pointed arches of the Early English S arcade contrast with the wider flat-topped arches of those of the Perpendicular period of the N arcade. Thomas Baron (d.1525) paid for the building of the N aisle and his initials are on one of the medieval bench ends. One small window in the chancel holds all that remains of the medieval glass, thanks to a visit by the tireless William Dowsing. He was appointed by Parliament in 1643 to destroy whatever might be offensive to the Puritans. He kept a diary and here in Comberton he wrote that he broke down "a crucifix, 69 superstitious pictures .... 36 cherubims, and gave order for the remainder, with the steps, to be taken down". Villagers rescued some of the angels' wings and defiantly nailed them back in the N aisle.

CONINGTON Nr. Cambridge *St. Mary* [D6]

Approaching through the large, well-tended churchyard, the progress of different building periods of St. Mary's can be seen: the tower is 14th century, nave 18th century, chancel rebuilt in 1870. Inside, extensive restoration was lovingly carried out in recent years by a dedicated priest-in-charge, an indefatigable church warden and many equally tireless villagers. One of the most impressive collections of monuments in East Anglia commemorates a long line of Lords of the Manor: the Cottons, Askhams, Hattons and Gardeners. Grinling Gibbons signed his elaborate memorial to young Robert Cotton who died in 1697, aged 14. The chancel is dimly lit through the Victorian glass. One of the four bells is reputed to be the oldest in the county, *c*.1365. A contented, peaceful place.

CONINGTON Hunts. *All Saints* [B4]

An important example of the mature Perpendicular style of the late 15th century. The Cotton family were Lords of the Manor from 1460 and this large church, then dedicated to St.Mary, was probably largely built by Thomas Cotton (d.1505). Many fine monuments including one to David, King of Scotland, whose family were Lords of the Manor here during the 12th and early 13th centuries; many Cotton and Heathcote memorials; also a

Conington

remarkable very early marble effigy, *c*.1300, of a young Franciscan. Beside the 13th century font lie memorials to a brother and sister who died in infancy. A detailed guide is provided by the Redundant Churches Fund which now cares for All Saints.

COTON *St. Peter* [E7]

A lovely village church with two small late medieval porches. Two small round-arched windows survive from the Norman building; also the massive font with each side decorated with primitive designs. Few of the medieval craftsmen are known, but here inside the tower on the S wall is written in Latin 'Andrew

Swynow... began the arch on St. Wulstan's day 1481'. The woodwork is largely Jacobean, and the lock on the screen doors is dated 1622. The organ was moved to its present position 20 years ago and now stands, cheerfully repainted, in the S aisle. Memorial to Dr. Andrew Downes (d.1627) one of the translators of the King James Bible and "the foremost Greek scholar of Europe ...." The tower is one of five in the area built during a period of forty years about 1400, possibly designed by the same master mason; the others are Barton, Caldecote, Hatley St. George and Knapwell.

COTTENHAM *All Saints* [E6]

A splendid building complete with battlements. A gale destroyed most of the tower and it was rebuilt in pale pink brick from 1617-19. The bulbous pinnacles were added at this time. Many of the donors' names can be seen on the S face, and a sundial warns us that "Time is Short". Many gargoyles including a shaggy-maned lion. The tall Perpendicular windows and large clerestory make for a light interior. In the chancel, the lovely 15th century piscina with shelf above and triple sedilia are enhanced by a delicate quatrefoil frieze. The bench ends, by a local craftsman, are a 19th century addition.

COVENEY *St. Peter-ad-Vincula* [E4]

The church stands on a ridge, almost hidden by trees. The nave and chancel are mostly 13th century; the tower, with its open base, a little later. The interior is a little gem. Athelstan Riley was Patron of the living here and generously endowed the church with its present furnishings. His initials are carved on the rood screen (1896). Fine stained glass in E window by Geoffrey Webb (1937), his work easily distinguished by his 'spider web' symbol. The reredos, *c.*1500, is of German origin. The pulpit (1706), with painted panels of the apostles, came from Denmark. In the nave some medieval benches remain and carved poppyheads include the keys of St. Peter and the cockerel. Fine views from both sides of the churchyard. An inscription on the lych gate commemorates those who gave their lives "to keep their country free from the chains of a foreign yoke". If you walk a little way N along the

Coveney

ridge you will understand why the majestic Ely cathedral is called the Ship of the Fens.

COVINGTON *St. Margaret* [A5]

A compact little church on the county's south-western edge. A fine example of a Norman door on the N wall with the carving of the tympanum looking almost as fresh as it must have done in the 12th century; another round-arched doorway in the S chancel wall. The font is Norman too with low decoration on the bowl and base; attractive modern font cover. More Norman fragments are built into the chancel wall. The S doorway, chancel S windows and piscina are all 13th century. Outside on the nave S wall is a blocked window which must have been inserted to throw light on the medieval rood screen. There is also evidence of an earlier chapel on the S side also, and the blocked archway remains.

CROXTON *St. James* [C7]

Once the centre of the small village but now stands alone following the landscaping of the park in the 18th century. Madingley and Wimpole are other examples of this fashion, largely due to the influence of Capability Brown. Late

Perpendicular tower with good, though crumbling, decoration. The interior is quite unspoilt. There are still two sofas in the family chapel. The servants' pews were to the W and the remaining pleasantly careworn benches are 15th century. Cromwell's troops are said to have been billeted here and perhaps took notice of the roundel in the SW window, warning the military not to steal the church plate. Most of the medieval glass has gone but large angels remain in the roof. Interesting churchyard with an ornate tomb of the Rev. William Cavendish Bentinck (d.1865) grandfather of the Queen Mother. A strange box-like stone remembers an "honest and valued servant ... 62 years in employment".

CROYDON *All Saints* [D8]
A simple unspoilt country church, but it is quite alarming to see the angle of the 14th century S arcade and walls. The large Norman font stands immediately inside the entrance. Niches in the S chapel on either side of the window and a little ogee-arched piscina. Sir George Downing, founder of Downing College (d.1749), is buried here. His grandfather, Sir Charles Downing, had an unsavoury career, serving Cromwell or the King as it best suited him. However, he is well known today: he leased a piece of land in London, built houses on it and gave his name to the street.

DIDDINGTON *St. Lawrence* [B6]
You must walk across fields to reach this interesting church. The chancel and N arcade are Early English and the lancet windows remain; the low-side window is early 14th century. The brick tower and porch were built during the reign of Henry VIII. This was a rare occurence during that troubled era when monasteries were being destroyed all over the country and little rebuilding was undertaken. Some lovely medieval bench ends survive too. Good 15th century stained glass and continental glass of a later date.

DODDINGTON *St. Mary* [D3]
The tower and nave are 14th century. The chancel is earlier and a large royal Coat of Arms dominates the N wall. Lovely angels in the medieval nave roof. Here also a window from the now demolished Benwick church has been reused. A famous rector here was Christopher Tye, musician to four monarchs. He composed for Henry VIII, Edward VI and Mary Tudor until he retired to Doddington during the reign of Elizabeth I. E window in N aisle is from the early school of William Morris, *c.*1865. Many 18th century headstones in the churchyard and the tall cross at the entrance stands on a 14th century base.

DOWNHAM-IN-THE-ISLE *St. Leonard* [F4]
A sturdy Norman tower and a wonderful doorway; the pointed arch from the late-Norman or Transitional period of the late 12th century. This leads on to the typical 13th century lancet windows and alternating (round and octagonal) arcades. The Coat of Arms of George III dominates the W end of the nave. In the N aisle hangs an 'Act of Parliament Clock' (so called because Pitt the Younger imposed a tax on clocks and watches in the late 18th century, and it became more economic to rely on public clocks). In the N aisle a chapel is dedicated to Ovin, steward to St. Etheldreda.

DRY DRAYTON *St. Peter and St. Paul* [D6]
The church was owned by Crowland Abbey from the 9th century until 1543. An attractive building standing at the edge of the village. The exterior is largely the result of 19th century rebuilding, though the 14th century style of the medieval church was followed. Very worn sedilia stand next to the chancel wall; perhaps the chancel was shortened resulting in the loss of the piscina. Weathered corbels, one with handsome moustache. The 19th century E window is dedicated to the Smith family; father and son were both rectors here. The glass is by Willement, who marked his work with his initials T.W. in a shield. Beautiful brass of Thomas Hatton and his wife, with their four sons and seven daughters, *c.*1540.

DULLINGHAM *St. Mary* [G7]
Very handsome N porch with a flushwork frieze, and two good gargoyles holding the down spouts; the frieze continues around the N aisle. The chancel still has the pointed arches of the 13th

century, but the rest of the church was built in various stages from 1399 to 1525. The large green marble pulpit (1903) comes as somewhat of a surprise. The font is dated 1622 but looks earlier. Several good monuments by Westmacott (father and son) to members of the Jeaffreson family. Lt.Gen. Jeaffreson, whose "heart teemed with kindness", died in 1824. Outside you can see the blocked priest's door in the chancel; also notice on the S side how strangely the tower buttress stands against the chapel. Several early 18th century headstones.

Bear   Boar   Lions.

Duxford - St Peter

DUXFORD *St. John* [E8]

No longer used as a parish church, it is now in the care of the Redundant Churches Fund; the wall-paintings being gradually restored by students from the Courtauld Institute. The strongly carved moulding of the doorway is Norman, but the unusually shaped cross may be earlier, as it resembles those seen on Anglo-Saxon buildings. Inside, massive Norman piers support the crossing tower. Graffiti here also, including a 'swastika pelka', or Solomon's Knot, which Mrs. Pritchard has found to be common in many churches.

DUXFORD *St. Peter* [E8]

Attractive flint church with 12th century tower and some windows remaining from the Norman period. The chancel is almost as large as the nave and was embellished with much tiling during the restoration in 1883. The stone faces of the corbels in the nave roof are quite startling, with a fiendish grinning boar and a far from benevolent lion. In the Lady Chapel the two modern, brightly painted saints, stand comfortably in their 15th century niches supported by medieval angels.

EASTON *St. Peter* [B5]

Perpendicular broach spire similar to that at Ellington. The porch has stone seats, windows which are 'framed' with arcading on the inside, and a stringcourse matching that of the tower, all very similar to the porch at Buckworth and to some extent like Old Weston. Fragments of a Norman window have been built into the N wall. In the S aisle more 12th century sculpture and what may be a later medieval Consecration Cross. A simple oak rood screen of the 15th century. The nave roof is prominently dated 1630. Above N door are listed the Charitable Donations of 1826.

EATON SOCON *St. Mary* [B7]

Fire destroyed the interior of the medieval building in 1930, though much of the outer shell remained. Funds were swiftly found and this fine new church, designed by Sir Albert Richardson, was consecrated in 1932. It is light and airy and has impressive woodwork throughout, especially the reredos and stalls. The loft above the elegant rood screen is reached by a spiral staircase in the N aisle. Some of the old corbels remain in the N aisle, but elsewhere you are watched by the 20th century faces of local people involved with the rebuilding. The square font is Norman, with typical decoration of intersecting arches.

ELLINGTON *All Saints* [B5]

A slender Perpendicular tower with battlements and happily weathered gargoyles. The E and N chancel windows are all *c.*1290, the tracery was restored by Sir Gilbert Scott in 1863. The aisle, clerestory nave and N porch are all Perpendicular. On a bright day the interior is flooded with light and the 15th century carvings in the roofs can be appreciated - apostles and angels with outstretched wings. Notice also the altar rails and benches, which are the work of Victorian craftsmen.

Elm

ELM *All Saints* [E2]

Wonderful Early English tower, with three tiers of blank arcading and lancets of the 13th century; you need to stand away to appreciate the breadth of the base. The W doorway has an earlier rounded arch. Inside, the size of the tower arch is quite breathtaking. Practically all the interior is Early English including the unusually early clerestory windows. Notice the old roofline above the tower arch. The 13th century string course continues in the chancel where the windows have been heavily restored. The lovely nave roof is late medieval and names of the churchwardens are written in the N aisle roof as a reminder of a restoration in 1620.

ELSWORTH *Holy Trinity* [D6]

As you enter by the N porch, the high arcades and imposing tower create a feeling of great space. The chancel, although much restored in the last century, must be the oldest part. The piscina and sedilia echo the delicate tracery of the windows, all late 13th century Decorated. There is one distinctive Perpendicular window in the chancel, and below it a small low-side window. The handsome stalls are late 15th century, early Tudor, and have unusual lockers under the bookrests. The large reredos has been removed from behind the high altar and is now at the W end of the nave.

ELTISLEY *St. Pandionia and St. John* [C7]

The elegant spire can be seen from afar. Most of the church is Early English, 13th century, including the very fine doorway with dogtooth ornament of about 1200. The chancel was demolished in 1841 and was rebuilt using a yellow brick. St. Pandionia is thought to have been a daughter of a Scottish prince; she died at a Benedictine nunnery nearby in 904. Her body was translated into the church in 1344 and many miracles occurred. St. Pandionia's Well stood outside the chancel until the 16th century when it was demolished for being used for "superstitious purposes".

ELTON *All Saints* [A3]

A particularly fine late Perpendicular tower, *c.*1500, with quatrefoil friezes, a large sundial and gargoyles all around. The chancel arch, *c.*1270, has nailhead decoration. Some 16th century benches, some with linenfold panelling and in the N aisle an 18th century German vestment cupboard. Much fine glass of the Arts and Crafts era and later. Several by William Morris and Burne-Jones, with marvellous colours in the W window of the S aisle. The Te Deum or All Saints E window is by Clayton & Bell, 1893. Many memorials to members of the Proby family, including an Admiral, Colonel, Lord Lieutenant and others. The pulpit was the gift of Fr. Faber, when he was the incumbent here, before he seceded to Rome and founded the Brompton Oratory.

ELY *St. Mary* St. Mary's Street [F4]
Superb N doorway, thought to have been made in the nearby monastery workshop during the late 12th century. Tall arcades dominate the elegant interior and lead to the Early English chancel. The chapel has an interesting window showing the martyrdom of St. Edmund and St. Etheldreda and a detailed picture of the cathedral. For another superb view of the octagon and roofs of the cathedral, walk around to the garden to the S side. A Saxon font and ancient coffin stand here, in front of the handsome hexagonal parish room, built in 1985.

Ely – St Mary

ELY *St. Peter* Broad Street [F4]
The widow of Canon Edward Boyer built this church as a memorial to her husband; it was dedicated in 1890. This was then a densely populated area of Ely, with much river traffic as well as therailway which had arrived in 1845. A very neat building, lovingly cared for by a small congregation. There is a beautiful painted Rood Screen, by Sir Ninian Comper; angels either side of

the Rood Group are balanced delicately on wheels, a device often used by Comper to indicate their ceaseless motion.

Etton

ETTON *St. Stephen* [B2]
St. Stephen's has changed little since it was built and is a superb example of the Early English period. The 13th century tower has a frieze of little heads and a horizontal sheila-na-gig figure. On the N wall of the chancel the outline of an earlier chapel and its piscina can still be seen. The long, narrow chancel has 13th century Y-tracery windows with trefoils. Over the low-side window is a lovely flowing arch; it must be a little later though it is still not quite the ogee of the Decorated period. It could be the same date as the early 14th century quatrefoil windows of the clerestory. There is a plain octagonal font with 17th century cover. Careful restoration was carried out in the 19th century; but the tiled chancel floor inserted at this time has considerably shortened the priest's doors. Medieval wall-paintings have recently been uncovered in the S aisle.

EYE *St. Matthew* [C2]

Building of this cruciform church began in 1836 using the Early English style. It was designed by George Basevi, who died after falling from scaffolding on Ely Cathedral. A spire was added some ten years later, but was removed *c.*1982/3 and replaced by the saddle-back you see now. The lancet windows are filled with Victorian glass; the E window, 1863, by Gibbs. The font and piscina are from the original 14th century building.

Eynesbury

EYNESBURY *St. Mary* [B7]

Many fine things to admire in this rather plain brown cobble building, outwardly in the Perpendicular style. The Early English doorway opens on to a much earlier interior. The round piers of the N arcade are Norman, *c.*1100. The stoup was once the base of the medieval town cross of St. Neots. The early 15th century carving of the bench ends is quite superb and is known locally as the Eynesbury Zoo. There are human heads, a camel and a pig with an orange in his mouth. Then the pulpit - a beautiful example of late 17th century work and may have come from a London workshop influenced by Christopher Wren. A memorial in the nave floor to 'The Eynesbury Giant', said to be the tallest man in England. The tower was struck by lightning and rebuilt in 1687 but the Norman arch survives. In the vestry are memorials to former rectors - the passing of the Revd. William Palmer was "regretted by all classes", thanks perhaps to his generosity in regularly distributing a pint of brandy to his parishioners. A detailed account in the porch of a Colonel's numerous battles and wounds in the Napoleonic wars: no wonder he called his son William Wellington Waterloo.

FARCET *St. Mary* [C3]

Walk round outside the tower to see the 12th century rounded lancets in the lower stages; it was completed about 100 years later at the same time as the nave and S arcade. Low-side window on N wall of chancel - they are more often found in the S wall. The rare 13th stone seat resembles those at Houghton and Stanground; here there is an original flower-like design on one arm, the other is a more recent copy. An older roofline can be seen on the E face of the chancel arch. The N aisle, roof and clerestory date from a restoration in the 1850s but some medieval carvings remain. Handsome Early Renaissance pulpit with linenfold decoration.

FEN DITTON *St. Mary* [E6]

A rowing eight tops the weathervane, oars stand in the nave and further links with the river Cam are found in the new (1989) W window. It recalls Wick Alsop (d.1987) who for many years, at the Annual Oarsmen's Service, would read a passage from "The Pilgrim's Progress." The tower is 13th century, N

Fen Ditton

35

aisle and chancel are Decorated (early 14th); the rest mainly 15th century Perpendicular. Cole's records tell of glass in the E window with the arms of Bishop Hotham (1316-37); so it could be true that Alan of Walsingham, creator of the Octagon at Ely c.1330, was responsible for building the scissor-beam chancel roof here. The font is late 14th century, with mutilated arms of Bishop Arundel (1374-88) and the arms of Ely (3 crowns); it came from the Cathedral in 1881. Major restoration was carried out in the late 19th century and much of the glass is from this period. In S aisle Kempe has signed his window with his usual wheatsheaf motif, but unusually he has put it at the very top. Outside there are some good early 18th century headstones with skulls, weeping angels and swags of roses. Read of the Willys family in the chancel - Ann, mother of 13 children, died in 1685 and thirty years later it seems that four generations died in a very short period of time.

FEN DRAYTON St. Mary [D6]

Lovely little brown cobbled church. The low tower has windows and bell-openings in the Decorated style of the early 14th century, and the various stages of building, using slightly different material, can easily be seen. The tiny window in the N wall of the chancel is something of a mystery; perhaps an anchorite or hermit had a cell here and thus was able to see the high altar; from the inside it looks like a squint. Pevsner suggests it may be Saxon. Two box pews are preserved in the chancel, but sadly little remains of the rood screen though one of the delicately carved panels now hangs in the S aisle.

FENSTANTON St. Peter and St. Paul [D6]

Turn at the King William IV and make your way past thatched cottages to this neat and attractive church. The chancel, surprisingly large and with an impressive E window, was built by William of Longthorne, rector here from 1345-1352. Much of the remainder is of the later Perpendicular period. Elegant monument with an eloquent inscription to Capability Brown, the illustrious landscape gardener. He was lord of the manor here and died in 1783. The dark wooden roofs of both aisles have many handsome

angels, now without wings, but still clutching their once brightly painted shields. Before you leave the village, look at the little brick jail house, built about 1600.

Fletton

FLETTON St. Margaret [B3]

A peaceful churchyard despite the surrounding bustle of Peterborough. Late 13th century, Early English, tower with broach spire. Rather severe square windows on S aisle and clerestory are 17th century. It is the Anglo-Saxon sculptures that are the great treasure here. Until quite recently (1981) the lovely frieze now set safely behind the altar was built into the E buttress of the chancel. The work is thought to be early 9th century. On the S wall of the chancel are two carvings of Saints, perhaps

Norman, early 12th century. We are fortunate that the church is standing at all today, as arsonists almost destroyed it in 1983. The charred pages of the Visitors' Book show where they defiantly wrote "The Destroyers", but the blaze was seen in time and the fire was contained.

FOLKSWORTH *St. Helen* [B3]

Dedicated to the mother of Constantine, the first Christian Emperor. Delightful unspoilt churchyard, filled with cowslips in the spring, where William Cockerill "waiteth for a glorious resurrection" beneath an unusually early headstone of 1611. Walk around to the N to find a small Norman doorway with what looks like a portcullis above it; this in fact should be more grandly known as a

Folksworth

tympanum of 'gridiron and pellets'. A gargoyle of particularly vindictive appearance faces you at eye-level at the porch. The massive Norman arch quite dominates the nave; the chancel beyond is a product of Victorian rebuilding and zealous restoration in the 1850s.

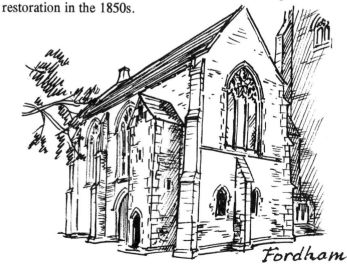

Fordham

FORDHAM *St. Peter* [G5]

The pride of this medieval church is the two-storied Lady Chapel in the Decorated style, early 14th century. Once quite separate from the church, but now joined to the N aisle. Round-headed Norman windows remain here but most are 15th century Perpendicular. Early English chancel, 13th century, with lancets and typical dogtooth ornament on the chancel arch. The medieval stalls here, some with misericords, may have come from Fordham Abbey. It is the wall-paintings which really stand out - not at all the medieval ones you might expect, but a happy blend of Edwardian colour on medieval stone. The artists were two sisters, Edith and Minnie Townsend, who completed the work in 1905.

FOWLMERE *St. Mary* [E8]

A handsome flint cruciform church. A fine string-course of ballflowers ornaments the N transept as this was, and remains, the 'show' side which faces the village street. A massive door opens on to an impressive interior. The chancel is Early English with original double piscina and low-side window. The large memorial on N wall is to William Mitchell (d.1745). Mr. Mitchell was related to the Bennetts of Babraham, two of whom have a remarkable 17th century monument. The E window here is by Clayton &

Fowlmere

Bell who also made the prettier window by the font. The transepts are later, and the ogee arch of the Decorated period takes over in the niches, though no statues remain. The ogee arch is repeated in the elegant rood screen. Part of a Norman capital can be seen in the porch but little survives of the earlier church.

Fulbourn

FOXTON *St. Laurence* [E8]

Three distinct types of window to be seen as you approach. Three 13th century Early English lancets of the chancel, the Decorated windows of the N aisle a little later, and the 15th century Perpendicular in the clerestory. Indulgences were granted here for rebuilding in 1456. Marvellous interior with screen and wooden chancel arch, all much restored. The upper doorway of the rood stair indicates how far forward was the roodloft. The 15th century chancel roof has carved wooden angels bearing shields. A particularly destructive visit from William Dowsing in 1644 resulted in the church becoming a "neglected wreck" during the next 30 years. Happily subsequent restorations have been sympathetic and St. Laurence still gives a good idea of a village church before the Reformation.

FRIDAY BRIDGE *St. Mark* [E2]

An alarming sight, as the tower leans at a dramatic angle and appears to be taking the west front with it. Villagers are undismayed as apparently this happened soon after it was built in 1864 (designed by J.B. Owen). Victorian glass, one window signed Alex Gibbs, London, 1868.

FULBOURN *St. Vigor* [F7]

An unusual dedication to a 6th century missionary who became Bishop of Bayeux (514-538) and converted many violent Norsemen to the Christian faith. A second church once shared this graveyard, while serving a separate parish. All Saints tower collapsed during a storm on Trinity Sunday 1766; a private Act of Parliament allowed it not to be repaired. The churches almost touched each other, closer even than the two you may still see at Swaffham Bulbeck; if you can find the tomb of Elizabeth March you will be inside what was once All Saints. The pulpit you see now, with the beautiful panels of St. John and St. Elizabeth of Hungary, may well be early 14th century. The panels are thought to have come from the rood screen of All Saints. Notice the lovely carving of owls and other birds, rose hips, bluebells and little human faces supporting delicate arches. In the chancel a tomb recess with cadaver is a memorial to a 15th century rector. Large brass (1377-86) in chancel floor. Several other good brasses; don't miss those let into the wall in the S aisle, near the splendid 17th century monument to Mr. Wood and his lady.

GAMLINGAY *St. Mary* [C7]

Marvellous cruciform church of local russet-coloured stone which was quarried just outside the churchyard. A stately 15th century exterior with battlements and gargoyles. A small lancet remains in the N aisle from an earlier building. Elaborate two-storey vaulted N porch and tall single-storey S porch. Light floods the interior, where you will find an Early English font of *c.*1200 and a fine Rood Screen of the late 14th century. The chancel has triple Decorated sedilia, the piscina perhaps a little later; the roof holds large angels with wings outstretched. In the S aisle notice the tall narrow cupboard, used since medieval times, to hold the

processional banners. In the N transept, a little squint is set quite low down, but would once have given a good view of the high altar. Interesting graffiti throughout. Several of the choir stalls, *c.*1442, have misericords, and the panelling behind retains some original colour.

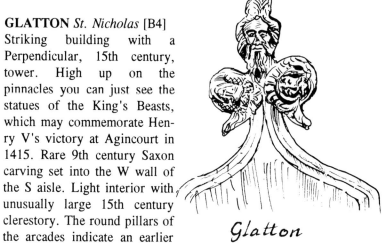

Gamlingay

GIRTON *St. Andrew* [E6]
Various building stages can be seen in the differing colours and types of materials used. Before you go in, notice the base of the tower: it is rectangular, not square and the lower part, with herringbone pattern, was built in the 11th century. On the tower E wall can be seen the faint outline of the roof of the Norman nave. A 20th century statue of St. Andrew stands above the entrance to the medieval porch; it has an upper room which may have been added at the same time as the clerestory and battlements. The N wall of the chancel has two blocked windows watched over by a particularly cheerful lion. There is a strange blocked window in the E wall of the chancel

too. In the N aisle hangs an imposing list of Donations and Benefactions dated 1853; the rector seemingly more generous than his parishioners.

GLATTON *St. Nicholas* [B4]
Striking building with a Perpendicular, 15th century, tower. High up on the pinnacles you can just see the statues of the King's Beasts, which may commemorate Henry V's victory at Agincourt in 1415. Rare 9th century Saxon carving set into the W wall of the S aisle. Light interior with unusually large 15th century clerestory. The round pillars of the arcades indicate an earlier

Glatton

date, about 1200, though they would have been lower then. Fine poppyheads on the benches, particularly the man carrying a woman's head under each arm. Several wall-paintings *c.*1500 and a tall, elegant rood screen.

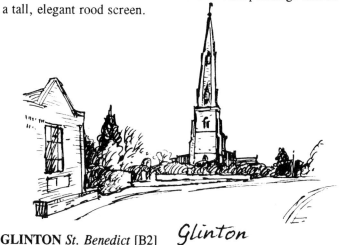

GLINTON *St. Benedict* [B2] *Glinton*
Beautiful spire (*c.*1510), very tall and slender, with pronounced entasis, rising from the battlements of the 15th century tower. The

gargoyles on the S clerestory are worth a mention. There are three quite ordinary ugly faces and one "reverse view", supposedly put there by the disgruntled mason when his wages remained unpaid. Two 14th century figures in the porch, the lady still elegant despite her worn appearance; opposite is a forester with his horn. Inside, traces of wall-painting survive on either side of the chancel arch. Notice the 19th century carving of bench ends with all manner of beasts and angry faces. The poet John Clare, who lived in nearby Helpston, attended the school in the Lady Chapel here in the early 1800s.

GODMANCHESTER St. Mary the Virgin [C5]

A stately church built for a large and prosperous medieval town. A rare Saxon Mass Dial is set into a buttress on the S chancel wall. The Norman church had a central tower and an outline of an earlier roof can just be seen above the chancel arch. Major rebuilding took place in the 13th century; the church was lengthened and the tower built at the W end. In the late 14th century the wealthy merchants again enlarged their church. The

Godmanchester

tower fell into disrepair and was rebuilt in 1623 using much of the original 13th century material. Small 14th century N porch, but enter through the more elaborate S porch. Inside, much remains of the Early English building. The 15th century choir stalls may be from Ramsey Abbey; some have beautifully carved misericords: a fox and goose, a rabbit and a deer rubbing its nose; the initials W.S. refer to William Stevens, vicar here 1470-1481. Several windows by Kempe and one by William Morris and Co., 1911. In the S chapel the reredos and altar rails are by Martin

Travers, who is buried in the churchyard. Many interesting headstones and tombs, particularly that of Mary Ann Weems who was murdered by her husband in 1819.

GOREFIELD St. Paul [E1]

An attractive flint church built in the Early English style, thanks almost entirely to the energies of the Revd. Andrew Beck, rector here from 1870 to 1901. The chancel, 1903, is dedicated to his memory. There is a handsome stone pulpit and oak lectern in the nave. The building is beautifully maintained and stands in a pleasant churchyard.

GRAFHAM All Saints [B6]

An unusual tower that becomes octagonal, and then has little 17th century pinnacles. The single bell dates to c.1400. The body of the church is mainly late 13th century, All Saints would then have been surrounded by woodland, but since the 1960s the large open space of the Grafham Water reservoir has quite altered the landscape. A quiet simple church but with a particular welcome about it. Chancel and N arcade remain from the Early English period. The S arcade, and the font, came a little later, in the Decorated style. Interesting memorials to members of the Puckle family.

GRANTCHESTER St. Andrew and St. Mary [E7]

Before entering, walk round to the S porch; beside it you will see evidence of much earlier buildings: a small Saxon window and interlace panels, Norman zigzag patterns, and two little 12th century faces. The tower can be dated by one of the shields on the lower window, that of Bishop Fordham of Ely, 1388-1426. The 15th century nave is rather gloomy but the chancel is quite spectacular. Pevsner suggests it may have been the work of craftsmen from the Lady Chapel workshop at Ely. It is certainly a wonderful example of the Decorated period: the ogee arch is used everywhere. An elaborate tomb recess in the N wall is surely that of the donor. There is also a large Norman font and a Jacobean pulpit. Corpus Christi College has been Patron here since 1380; their Coat of Arms, featuring the pelican (a symbol of

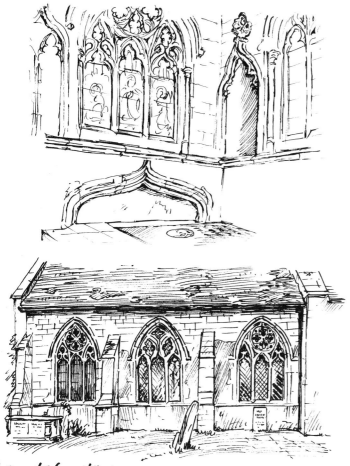

Grantchester

self-sacrifice) and lilies (purity) can be seen in the chancel and churchyard.

GRAVELEY *St. Botolph* [C6]

A unpretentious welcoming church, its chancel still lit by candlelight. Four cheerful little gargoyles greet you above the W door. Outside you can see what remains of the N aisle, perhaps taken down in the 18th century when the Rev. Henry Trotter undertook major restorations and "rebuilt and beautified the chancel". He died in 1766 and his memorial, telling of his generosity, is in the chancel. A more recent memorial to those who served with the Pathfinder Force at RAF Graveley in World War II. A picture dated 1748 shows a S porch and very different windows in E chancel wall. Read the memorial on the S wall of the chancel to Mary Warren; when only two years old, her family brought her back to England from India. She survived the journey, including crossing Egypt by camel, only to die at the rectory here at the age of three.

GREAT ABINGTON *St. Mary* [F8]

Approached down a long lane, beyond the thatched cottages in open fields. A flint and rubble church, mostly 13th century; with a group of three lancet windows in the tower and more lancets in the chancel. A later addition is the small window inserted to throw light on the rood screen. The rood loft has now long gone, but the worn steps which once led up to it remain. In the chancel, Sir William Halton (d.1639) rests resignedly on his elbow. He lies facing the organ with its striking case of dull reds and golds. The font is partly built into the pier of the tower arch.

GREAT CHISHILL *St. Swithin* [E9]

Beautifully situated in a lovely part of the county. Mainly built of flint. The porch was once two-storeyed; the staircase remains and the outline of the upstairs doorway. The base of the tower and the chancel arch are early 14th century but curiously they are not in line with the present nave. Beside this rather small chancel arch is an unusually broad squint. The organ, early 19th century, is by G.M.Holditch, who built the pedal organ in Lichfield Cathedral. There is a large graffito of two keys.

GREAT EVERSDEN *St. Mary* [D7]

The church was struck by lightning in 1466. An Indulgence was given in the same year for its rebuilding and work was carried out at the end of the 15th century, and much of the old material was reused. The piscina may also date from this time. Lovely timber porch dated 1636 and the pulpit is perhaps of slightly earlier date. Two misericords in the chancel, one with the arms of the

Beauchamp family. Admire the lovely modern design for an altar cloth, using local wild flowers.

GREAT GIDDING *St. Michael* [B4]

Great Gidding

As you approach, notice the windows in the chancel - good examples of the three different styles: Early English (central, triple lancets); Decorated (to the left, early 14th), and the larger Perpendicular window on the right. The S doorway, 1250, is perhaps the earliest part, but the nave and chancel, with lancets, are still 13th century. By 1400 the church was almost as you see it now, with clerestory, aisles and porch. The chancel boasts a particularly fine Decorated piscina, a Communion Rail of 1640. On the S wall is a wooden panel, dated 1614; on it is a remarkable word square such as was used by the first Christians in Rome. Fearsome gargoyles on N nave and smiling cherubs on some of the 18th century headstones in the churchyard.

GREAT GRANSDEN *St. Bartholomew* [C7]

An impressive church with grand battlements and startling gargoyles. Almost entirely in the Perpendicular style of the 15th and 16th centuries. Inside there are more handsome carved figures and bosses in the roof. In the chancel is a beautiful 15th century piscina, complete with shelf. Barnabas Oley (1602-1686) was the much loved rector here for 53 years, although his royalist connections forced him to flee north for some years. He was a great admirer of George Herbert and published many of his poems. The carillon and chimes were added to the splendid clock to honour his 50th year in the parish. The lych gate is a memorial to those who died in the Great War and a remarkable stained glass window was given in 1989 in memory of those that died flying from Gransden air field during World War II.

GREAT PAXTON *Holy Trinity* [C6]

Approaching from the north, the church appears quite low and sits comfortably into the landscape; it gives little preparation for the breathtaking height and space of the interior. This was a Minster church, built *c.*1020 and is said to be "the most ambitious building of the 11th century". Pevsner describes the N transept arch as being "thrown across at a height unparalleled in early English architecture". It is all quite spectacular and certainly worth a detour. Notice the bulbous capitals and the huge stones used in the wall-like piers to the E of the nave. The simple

Great Paxton

grandeur of it all will justify any time spent looking for the key. The chancel is 13th century with original piscina and double sedilia. The iron hinges and strap work on the S door are also the work of 13th century craftsmen.

GREAT SHELFORD *St. Mary* [E7]
A Norman church once stood here, but it was entirely rebuilt between 1396 and 1411 at the expense of Thomas Patesely, rector at St. Mary's and also Archdeacon of Ely. His brass lies in the chancel. A very fine two storey porch, and among the bosses in the roof is the pelican (symbol of piety) and a Green Man too. In 1798 part of the tower collapsed, together with the five bells; interesting inscriptions on the tower S wall date from the rebuilding. Delicate Parclose screen in N aisle. The rood screen has two more little Green Men facing the E window - was it supposed to face the other way? Splendid chancel roof with large bosses and much gilding, and the hammerbeams of the nave roof are supported by eight, now wingless, angels. Above the chancel arch, the painting of the Last Judgement or 'Doom', *c.*1400, is one of the finest in the country and probably dates from Patesely's building. A damned soul can be seen clutching at St. John's robe.

GREAT STAUGHTON *St. Andrew* [B6]
A very dignified church in a lovely setting, full of interest inside and out. Nothing remains of the church mentioned in the Domesday Survey but rebuilding began in the late 13th century; the aisles, porch and clerestory were added during the next 200 years. The pinnacled tower with two handsome quatrefoil friezes was added *c.*1470 and its buttresses obscure the aisles' W windows. Very unusually, the sanctus bell survives above the E wall of the nave. The N chapel, *c.*1455, contains many good monuments. On N chancel wall to the Dyers, one of whom was Lord Chief Justice; opposite is a memorial to the Conyers' infant son and daughter, watched over by cherubs. In the S aisle Valentine Wauton lies with his head on a red and gold pillow - he married Oliver Cromwell's sister, and was one of the regicides: his story is here for all to read. Also memorials and a window to members of the Duberly family, long associated with the village.

Great Shelford

Great Shelford: Screen and pulpit.

GREAT STUKELEY *St. Bartholomew* [C5]
A lovely position with panoramic views of the surrounding countryside from the churchyard: it is said that seven spires can be seen from here on a clear day. Of the original Norman church only fragments remain, now set into the walls. The arcades are late 12th century or early 13th, the Transition period from Norman to Early English. Only one pier has typical Early English 'stiff-leafed' decoration, from the same period as the lancets in the

chancel. Don't miss the truly splendid corbels in the tower. Also notice the medieval mason's use of recycled materials: old coffin stones were reused here when building the clerestory. Stand in S aisle and look N; at the top right hand corner of the easternmost window. (Somewhat complicated to find but certainly unusual.)

GREAT WILBRAHAM *St. Nicholas* [F7]
Walk round the outside first to appreciate fully this large cruciform church, built mainly during the Early English period of 13th century. Three tall lancet windows and one small round-headed Norman window on the N wall. To the S, the chancel has one flat-headed Perpendicular window and remains of another lancet. There is a substantial 15th century tower, with battlements and pinnacles. The lovely flint porch has seats either side and the grand S doorway has good examples of dogtooth ornament. The font is earlier and would have stood in the Norman church; it also has ornate decorations, each side a 'sampler' of 12th century decoration. The 14th century chequerboard painting on the crossing arches is still bright enough to give us an idea of the strong colours in medieval churches.

GUILDEN MORDEN *St. Mary* [C8]
The elegant spire can be seen from afar. The exterior of this large church seems to be entirely in the 15th century Perpendicular style. Inside, however, the nave is in the Decorated style of the 13th century; part of the S arcade a century earlier. The beautiful rood screen is a rarity, a blending of two or three 14th century designs. Much of the paintwork may be original: St. Edmund is shown with the crown and arrows of his martyrdom; he was killed by the Danes in 870 for refusing to renounce his Christianity. The Bishop depicted is Erkenwald, brother of Etheldreda the foundress of Ely Cathedral. The inscription begins "In death's dark hour, Jesu have care of me...". The chancel is full of light from the Perpendicular windows and has a marvellous hammerbeam roof where four pairs of angels overlook the more earthly figures of the corbels below. The 12th century font has pretty scrolling decoration over the lip of the bowl.

Guilden Morden

GUYHIRN *The Puritan Chapel* [D2]
Over the doorway, inscribed in stone, is the date 1660, the year in which England reverted to a monarchy, following the death of Cromwell and the end of the Commonwealth. It is said to be a Puritan building but in fact may be a simple Anglican chapel. It is quite unspoiled and has happily escaped any over-enthusiastic restoration. No light or heat, a simple communion table and narrow uncomfortable pews to encourage concentration on lengthy sermons. Wooden hat pegs remain on the walls. It is now in the care of the Redundant Churches Fund and the Friends of Guyhirn Chapel of Ease.

GUYHIRN *St. Mary Magdalene* [D2]

Remains of a medieval church were discovered when foundations were dug in 1877. The "new" church was designed by Gilbert Scott, built in yellow brick in the Early English style. There is a pleasant timber porch and fine Victorian work throughout, with angels either side of the chancel arch. The church was consecrated in 1878. The lectern was carved by the wife of the original benefactor. There is a triple bell-turret and quite recently a memorial cross was erected in the churchyard.

HADDENHAM *Holy Trinity* [E5]

This fine medieval church was almost a ruin in the 19th century. A massive restoration took place about 1876 and the architect, R.R. Rowe, paid much attention to the original details. Walk round outside to the W wall of the tower: there is little room to admire the restored early 14th century work, with typical ballflower but also the dogtooth decoration which is more usually found in earlier 13th century work. St. Etheldreda's steward, Ovin, may have built a church in Haddenham in the 7th century. A replica of his memorial cross is here but you must go to Ely cathedral to see the original. It was found in the village in the 18th century, being used as a mounting block. The chancel floor has tiles depicting the ministry of Christ. 15th century brass to John Godfrey and his wife. A fine window engraved by David Peace, 1969.

HADDON *St. Mary* [B3]

A churchyard filled with headstones and flowers in almost equal profusion. Stand away from the W wall of the tower and you will see the faintest outline of the steep roof of the Norman church, which would have had a bellcote only. Inside, the elaborate chancel arch is of the early 1100s and one round-arched Norman window survives. Large lancet windows in the transepts and the arcades are all 13th century. 15th century wall painting above the chancel arch, and more paintings are hidden behind the white plaster walls.

HAIL WESTON *St. Nicholas* [B6]

A lovely church of cobbles, very different from its neighbours. It has a large tiled roof and a timber tower, covered in shingles, which is the only one in the county. Inside, look at the ancient timbers in the roof: roses are carved along the length of one. A lancet window in the chancel remains from the 13th century building. Only the lower half of the rood screen has survived, but the reredos was added as recently as 1963. Some medieval benches survive in the W end.

HAMERTON *All Saints* [B5]

A peaceful setting, with fields on two sides of the churchyard. A fine church, mostly Perpendicular, with battlements on both sides. The porch has 13th century windows which were perhaps reused as they appear to predate the porch itself. The S doorway and much of the interior date from the 1300s. Here is another church with two low-side windows, similar to those at Bury. The medieval roof has carved angels, apostles and central bosses. The large 15th century font stands on three steps. The hand-pumped organ is one of the treasures here. Monument in S aisle to poor Mawde Bedel, who bore 5 sons and 5 daughters before she died in 1597, aged 37.

HARDWICK *St. Mary* [D7]

The church is mainly 15th century and stands in a tree-lined churchyard. The tower is 14th century and an ogee arch on the W doorway is evidence that the building began at the beginning of the century while the Decorated style was in fashion. The chancel has few furnishings except a massive parish chest. No screen survives but the stair doors are unusually tall. Both chancel and nave have 15th century queen-post roofs. A memorial slab under the tower arch to Thomas Barron who died in 1762: his earlier namesake (d.1525), was a benefactor to the church at Comberton. Small patches of wall-paintings remain. A major restoration was carried out in 1987.

Harlton

HARLTON *Assumption of the Blessed Virgin Mary* [D7]
A common dedication in the Middle Ages but most survive today
as St. Mary. A splendid interior and an important example of the
transition between the Decorated and Perpendicular periods. Built
mainly during the second half of the 14th and into the first part of
the 15th century. The chancel is dominated by the superb E
window with canopied niches on either side. The stone reredos is
a happy blend of original niches which now hold figures of the 12
apostles carved in 1934 by H.J. Ellison, son of a former rector
here. A fine stone rood screen; few of these have survived.
William Cole, in the 18th century, described the Fryer monument
as "most beautiful and magnificent" and so it is to this day. Sir
Henry Fryer died in 1631 fighting a duel in Calais, so he kneels
with hand on sword, flanked by his father in doctor's robes and
his mother; his stepmother lies below.

HARSTON *All Saints* [E7]
Delightful situation with the River Rhee bordering the western
end of the churchyard. The sturdy battlements, porch and conical
stair turret give All Saints an air of importance as you approach
from the N; (the entrance is more usually to the S). If you walk
around to the S here you will notice that expensive battlements
were not wasted on the less public side. All Saints is largely the
result of 15th century building. Notice the typical lozenge-shape
piers; this N-S elongation is often found in arcades of the
Perpendicular period. There is a simple rood screen and a
Jacobean pulpit stands on a wine glass stem. Notice the small
transept in the N aisle, and also the unusually narrow aisles;
perhaps the result of 15th century rebuilding when the nave may
have been widened at the expense of the aisles. The chancel
andvestry were rebuilt in 1853. The present peal of six bells was
hung in 1937.

HARTFORD *All Saints* [C5]
A delightful setting on the riverbank. A timber church in Hartford
was referred to in the Domesday Survey. This was replaced by
the Normans and the arcades and massive font survive from their
building. The Norman style chancel arch is almost entirely the
work of Victorian craftsmen during a restoration in 1861;
unusually the arch is decorated on both sides. The tower was built
during the 15th century but restoration was needed in the late
1800s and six bells were hung. The highly decorative pulpit is a
lavish Victorian addition. In a corner of the churchyard is a
triangular pillar, set up in 1735 when earlier monuments and
headstones were moved to enable the burial ground to be reused.

HASLINGFIELD *All Saints* [E7]

A very striking 15th century tower with quatrefoil frieze at the base, embattled turrets and wooden spire. Both porches are 14th century, though the S porch was rebuilt in 1746 and the churchwardens' names can be seen on the roof. The interior is mainly Decorated but the dogtooth moulding is earlier. Stone faces everywhere and particularly fine 14th century roofs in both aisles, with delicate tracery. Interesting monuments in the chancel; that of Thomas Wenday, 1612, and his family was recently restored. It was returned to the church in 174 different pieces but now once again stands as a proud memorial to the physician to Elizabeth I. Works of art are still being created - look at the altar kneelers which are designed and worked by a parishioner in the very finest detail. Notice also the painted chancel roof, restored by a 19th century rector.

HATLEY St. GEORGE *St. George* [C7]

An unusual appearance since the chancel was pulled down in 1966. The tower is one of five in the area (the others are Barton, Caldecote, Coton and Knapwell) built during a forty year period about 1400, and possibly designed by the same master mason. The clear E window lights the delicately carved angels in the fine hammerbeam roof. Heraldic arms of the St. George family line the walls. Marble monument to Thomas Quintin, 1806, by E. Gaffin. A loving memorial to Elizabeth Quintin who died in 1801, 32 years before her grieving husband. Several brasses, including one of Baldwin St. George, 1425.

HAUXTON *St. Edmund* [E7]

As you approach the S doorway, notice the Mass dials on either side of the handsome Norman entrance. Once inside there is more evidence of the 12th century church, particularly the massive chancel arch.

Hauxton

Altar recesses on either side of the arch, c.1229. One of them holds the earliest surviving painting of St. Thomas Becket, dated about 1250, only 80 years after his martyrdom. The villagers must have taken trouble to hide it during the reign of Henry VIII, when an order was made in 1538 that all representations of Becket should be "put down or defaced".

HELPSTON *St. Botolph* [B2]

Saxon foundations of "long and short" work are reputed to support tower; total rebuilding of the tower c.1865 reused medieval material. Much of the early 13th century interior remains. The chancel with sedilia and piscina is somewhat later, about 1300; the low-side window retains its iron grating and perhaps the original hinges. One deep medieval squint remains. A modern version of the squint can be seen beside the organ: a television screen which gives a very clear picture of the high altar. What may be two stone bench ends remain on either side of the chancel, not unlike the arms of the stone seat in Farcet, but here are strange primitive heads and no simple star design. The mosaic tiles in the chancel floor may well have come from the Roman villa nearby. The interior is dominated by the E window of Christ in Majesty, by Francis W. Skeat (1983). Outside the S wall of the chancel is the tomb of John Clare, the "Peasant Poet". He was born in Helpston in 1793 and died in Northampton in 1864. His family are buried close by. There are many finely worked kneelers in the church and John Clare's house is shown on one of them.

HEMINGFORD ABBOTS *St. Margaret of Antioch* [C5]

The Abbots of Ramsey were Lords of the Manor here and the village is thus distinguished from the Hemingford which once belonged to the Grey family. There is a very fine steeple with battlements, turrets and gargoyles, which replaced an earlier central tower. The main body of the church is of brown cobbles except for the chancel, built rather surprisingly in yellow brick about 1800. The font, with its decoration of round Norman arches, survives from the 12th century building and the glass screen, engraved by David Peace, celebrates the church's millennium in 1974. The 15th century roof is full of angels, some clasping musical instruments, others with shields. The medieval St. Christopher barely survives, but the new St. Christopher, at the Heming Ford, was completed in 1978.

Hemingford Grey

HEMINGFORD GREY *St. James* [C5]

Beautifully situated on the banks of the Ouse. The rather curious design to the upper part of the tower is the result of a hurricane in 1741 which destroyed the spire. The base was levelled and eight large balls placed on the angles. The interior is spacious and light. The centre arch in the N arcade is practically all that remains of the original Norman building which also had a central tower, as did Hemingford Abbots. The chancel is later, mid 13th century and was lengthened when the central tower collapsed. Notice the elaborate Early English double piscina, of the same design as those at Jesus College, Histon, St. Ives and other local churches. Outside on the S buttresses are two medieval Scratch dials and a large painted 18th century sundial on the clerestory.

HEYDON *Holy Trinity* [E8]

Above the N doorway is the history of Holy Trinity - its founding, near-destruction and renewal. On the S side there is a massive door to the porch, which must have been the main entrance at one time, with an equally impressive lock. Notice also, beside the chancel arch, the worn steps of the clunch stairway which once led up to the rood loft. Much Victorian restoration in the chancel, and the highly coloured reredos would have been added at that time. After being hit by a bomb in the 2nd World War, the church was rebuilt in the 1950s, but this has not altered its ancient and welcoming feeling.

HILDERSHAM *Holy Trinity* [F8]

A lovely situation overlooking meadows leading down to the Granta. The 13th century tower has been considerably heightened in the past 100 years. The ladder is said to have been here since it was first constructed! The windows are filled with Victorian glass and at first make it difficult to appreciate the brightly coloured Victorian murals in the chancel. All was planned by two Goodwins - a father and son rectorship lasting 94 years. The work was carried out, about 1890, by Italian craftsmen working at Pampisford Hall. Four good brasses, all of the Paris family. The nave is surrounded by arms of Lords of the Manor. The Jesse window in N aisle is by Clayton and Bell, 1860.

HILTON *St. Mary Magdalene* [C6]

Lovely approach through tree-lined paths to this large and stately church. The tower is 14th century but the rest of the building is later. A once-beautiful niche of the Decorated period in the S aisle. Most of the glass is 19th century with two windows by Kempe. Outside on the green, look for the stone pillar marking the intricate grass maze that has been challenging visitors since it was first cut in 1660, the year of Charles II's restoration.

HINXTON *St. Mary and St. John* [E8]

The church dates back to 1150, but there may have been a church here as early as 1080. The lower part of the sturdy flint and rubble tower is Early English, but the upper stage and elegant spire is a 15th century addition. The S door was added at this time; notice the corbels, their faces rather worn - perhaps the 19th century porch was built to protect them? Inside the Victorian pews sit rather primly, many with their original half doors. The stairway beside the Jacobean pulpit lead to what must have been a particularly large rood loft. John of Gaunt's steward, Sir Thomas Skelton (d.1416) is remembered on a fine brass in the Lady Chapel. The Norman N doorway, now blocked, is better seen from the outside.

Histon

HISTON *St. Andrew* [E6]
A cruciform church. Outlines of earlier steeper roofs can be seen on the central tower. Inside, the entrance to the rather dark nave gives little suggestion of the splendid Early English transepts beyond; they are without question the finest in the county. The elaborate double piscinas in both transepts are just like those in Jesus College, and copied in several churches in the county. Pevsner

suggests that the designer of the Early English work here must have come from the lodge working at St. Radegund's Nunnery and Jesus College in the latter part of the 13th century. Elegant blank arcading continues around the walls. The chancel too is Early English, but rather over-restored by Gilbert Scott. A tall niche in the S transept once held a statue of St. Catherine but only her wheel survives. A large angel stoops under an eagle's talons to provide an unusual lectern. Stained glass in S transept by Clayton & Bell, 1872.

HOLME *St. Giles* [B4]
Records tell of a church here in the 12th century but the present building, by Edward Browning of Stamford, dates only to 1862. A pleasant interior in the Decorated style. In the chancel, a fine gilded reredos and a particularly large and handsome chandelier. In the 19th century an enterprising rector established a floating church from here to serve those living along the canals in the more remote areas of his large parish.

HOLYWELL CUM NEEDINGWORTH *St. John the Baptist* [D5]
There has been a church here since 969 and a major rebuilding in the 13th century resulted in this fine building. The chancel is a good example of the Early English period with double lancet windows. The tower came much later, in 1547, constructed from stones retrieved from Ramsey Abbey after the Dissolution. In the nave are carved wooden figures which were originally with others in the roof. The medieval Rood doorway in the chancel arch now opens on to a 20th century screen. Try to be here for the colourful annual Well Dressing Ceremony, held towards the end of June. Interesting churchyard with good headstones, one particularly nice 18th century one with an angel holding crowns and swags of roses.

HORNINGSEA *St. Peter* [E6]
A massive restoration was undertaken last century by the energetic Fr. Chapman, parish priest for 54 years, and less than a decade ago more major repairs were needed. Records tell of a

Minster church here in 9th century but nothing can be seen of it now. Enter through the 14th century porch: the two huge lions as gargoyles are still startling, though sadly worn. As recently as 1985 there was no electricity here but now there is a choice of oil lamps, candles or electric light, and no longer any need to hand-pump the organ. Several interesting features: the fine pulpit with sounding board *c.*1600; a strange wide pillar attached to the remains of a wall in S aisle; early 13th century font. No rood loft remains; however, a piscina 12ft above the floor is evidence that the rood gallery must have been substantial enough for a small altar. Few rood lofts had such altars and piscinas, though another example can be found at Maxey.

Horseheath

Horseheath

HORSEHEATH *All Saints* [G8]

Spare some time for All Saints. The building is 14th century but there was a church here earlier still. The interior is beautifully light and airy, thanks to the large Perpendicular windows. The medieval rood screen has a little of the original paintwork and roses still decorate the doorway to the roodstairs. The church was probably complete by about 1524, when money was left to complete the battlements. William Dowsing no doubt destroyed much stained glass and statues when he visited here in 1643. Major rebuilding was necessary in the 18th century and again in 1891. Very fine monuments to the Alingtons in the chancel. Also a lovely brass of Sir William Audley, 1365, who is watched over by an angel very similar to the medieval angels which have survived in the E window above him.

HOUGHTON *St. Mary* [C5]

Elegant brown cobbled church standing beside the narrow road leading down to the water mill. Unusual tower with octagon, battlements and stone spire. The pinnacles were badly damaged during the hurricane of 1741 when the spire at Hemingford Grey was blown into the river. The chancel is 14th century Decorated, and here is another very early double piscina, perhaps about 1300 (similar to piscinas at Histon, Arrington and Hemingford Grey). The rare stone seat in the chancel resembles those at Stanground and Farcet but with a small star-like rosette on the armrest. Read the epitaph beside the porch; similar verse is found on blacksmiths' memorials in other parts of the country.

HUNTINGDON *All Saints* [C5]

The church dominates the small market place and much of the 14th century building remains. Opposite the church, the Cromwell Museum retains the Norman arches and blind arcading of about 1190, when it was part of the Hospital of St. John; later a Grammar school where Oliver Cromwell and Samuel Pepys were both students. Cromwell was baptized in All Saints, and Mary Queen of Scots' body rested here in October 1612 on the way to Westminster. The N arcade is Early English, and unusually the tower is in the NW corner. Much Victorian glass; the W window of the N aisle shows Cranmer, George Herbert, Newton, Queen Victoria, Prince Albert, Handel and the Duke of Wellington too. The W window is by Kempe (look for his wheatsheaf symbol); the E by his successor Tower (his symbol is easy to remember). Musical angels are everywhere: outside the N doorway, inside on the choir stalls, on the lovely organ and in the painted roof of nave and chancel.

HUNTINGDON *St. Mary* [C5]

A very grand late-Decorated tower, built between 1380-90; some rebuilding was necessary in the 17th century and the names and initials of donors can be seen on the upper stages, and the dates 1672 and 1677. The W doorway is quite elaborate, a frieze of grotesque little faces and niches on either side. At the top is a quatrefoil frieze, battlements and pinnacles. The interior is largely 13th century with one rather alarming 'leaning' pillar in the S arcade. The chancel was originally much larger as can be seen by the position of the priest's door which is now "too near" the E end. The High Altar and rails are by Comper, 1920. Beside the pulpit a stone recalls R. Cromwell, father of the Protector.

Huntingdon-St Mary

ICKLETON *St. Mary* [E8]

Make a detour if necessary to see this church. In 1979 an arsonist almost succeeded in destroying it and the tower's painted ceiling was ruined. However, some good came of it all because it was during the restoration that the extensive wall-paintings were discovered. They were painted between the 12th and 14th centuries and executed in true fresco, though most of the linework has gone and we are left with the block colour. They give a marvellous idea of the brightness and colour enjoyed by the medieval worshipper. But first look at the church itself. The magnificent arcades and small clerestory windows remain from

Ickleton

IMPINGTON *St. Andrew* [E6]

Remains of the earlier Norman church can still be found: a small carved head on the S wall of the chancel and chevron markings on several stones. The timber porch is medieval and once inside you will marvel at the wall-painting of St. Christopher. Close by, in a delicate niche surrounded by twenty tiny rose bosses, is a modern carving of the Crucifixion. Modern craftsmen also created the oak chest, decorated with simple oak leaves, which stands in the chancel. Brass of John Burgoyn and his family, 1504. Recent restoration is nicely recorded on rain pipes.

ISLEHAM *St. Andrew* [G5]

Dedicated in 1331 and a lovely example of the Decorated period. The 500 year old lych-gate is said by Claude Messent to be the oldest in East Anglia. A grand two-storey porch with blank arcading opens onto the very fine nave. Major rebuilding in the 15th century resulted in the elaborate decoration above the arcades, filled with shields of the Peyton family. The unusually high clerestory and angel roof were given by Chrystofer Peyton in 1495; the S transept has recently been restored by his descendants. Several superb brasses, but especially that of Thomas Peyton, 1484, and his two elegant wives. There are a

the Early Norman building *c.*1100. Notice the unusual cushion capitals which are typical of the period. The four end columns may have come from a Roman building and perhaps stood in the Saxon church here. The arcades are partly faced with Roman tiles and the salmon pink colour of the mortar was achieved by the use of crushed Roman brick. A large Roman villa and basilica once stood close by and the red tile on the outside W wall of the tower is more evidence of the reuse of Roman materials. Several medieval poppyheads survive on the benches, notably St. Michael weighing the souls, and an ox, the symbol of St. Luke. The wall-paintings certainly deserve lengthy appreciation and the excellent Guide Book describes them in detail. Outside, carved medieval coping stones have been incorporated into the churchyard wall.

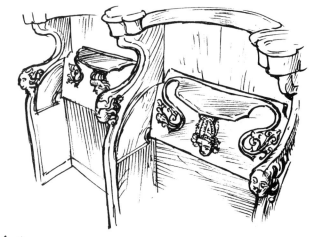

Isleham

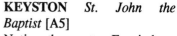

Isleham

large number of tombs, especially the two splendid six-poster Renaissance memorials to Sir Robert and Sir John Peyton. In the N transept read the memorial to Revd. Peachey Clerke, 1683. The piscina here is angled into the wall. No chancel arch remains but a little picture shows the rood gallery in place. Much to admire: brasses, misericords of *c.*1450 and lovely carved bench ends with poppyheads, shields and animals. Before you leave the village, notice the secularised 11th century Norman Priory Church; a lovely unspoiled example of the period with herringbone masonry and typical small windows.

KENNETT *St. Nicholas* [G6]

Someone at the little Post Office knows the whereabouts of the key. The church is hidden at the end of a long grassy lane. Almost entirely an Early English building with large triple lancets in chancel. A lovely little double piscina with slightly large Victorian decoration. The tower and N arcade are Perpendicular and the W window has attractive stained glass.

KEYSTON *St. John the Baptist* [A5]

Notice the pretty E window, trefoils in the circle beside the tulip-like tracery. Now walk around to the W face of the tower: the elaborate doorway and window are lovely examples of the early 14th century Decorated period; but the design of the broach spire is earlier, similar to other 13th century spires in the area. The reason is that, during a major rebuilding in 1882, the Early English style was preferred. Continue round to the N wall of the chancel, perhaps not so interesting but you can see the work of various masons over the centuries - old rooflines, a blocked doorway, an Early English lancet and a later Perpendicular window. Lively faces in stone and wood in the porch and nave roofs. The 13th century chancel has a fine piscina, sedilia and priest's door. In the N aisle lies a grim 15th century cadaver.

Keyston

Kimbolton

KIMBOLTON *St. Andrew* [A6]
This tower and broach spire was completed in the early 1300s; there is an unusual frieze of tiny heads at the top. Handsome S porch in Perpendicular style. Inside, the round piers of the S arcade may precede the alternating round and octagonal piers of the N arcade; a progression from the early to the late 13th century. There are marvellous figures in the aisle roofs and stone corbels in the chancel. The lovely medieval screens with painted panels are more often seen in Norfolk and Suffolk. There is much to see here: from Cromwellian bullet marks in the door to the delightful monument (1912) to Consuelo, Duchess of Manchester; Tiffany glass, 1902; a plaque commemorating the 379th Bomber Group of the US Air Force. The font may be Saxon or as late as the 12th century (Pevsner considered it to be "very uncouth").

KING'S RIPTON *St. Peter* [C5]
A simple early 14th century building. The tower was added a century later and has a very high interior arch. Later still the chancel was refaced and the porch added. The piscina comes from an earlier building and is probably about 1260. Large E window, reset by the Victorians. A memorial (1837) in the chancel, to a presumably harassed parson, remembers that "his lot, alas, was not so envious here."

KINGSTON *All Saints and St. Andrew* [D7]
The church was rebuilt following a disastrous fire in 1488. The outline of the earlier roof can still be seen on the E face of the tower. The rood screen and the extensive wall-paintings date from that "new" church. In the N aisle the painting of the Wheel shows the Seven Acts of Mercy with the "Laying out of the Dead" at the top; a particularly lively Devil watches from below. Victorian restoration usually raised chancel floors to enhance the importance of the altar; however, here you must step down into the chancel. Village lore says that it was the stabling of Cromwell's horses here that caused the floor to be so low. More paintings in the chancel and a monk can be seen between the S windows. The base of the font is delicately carved; perhaps it was once used as the bowl itself.

KIRTLING *All Saints* [G7]
Set quite apart from the village, on the Newmarket side of Kirtling Towers and not very easy to find, at the end of an unmarked lane. But a rewarding place to visit. A handsome Norman doorway, with a 12th century tympanum of Christ in Majesty; the iron strapwork may be almost as old. A small window to the W of the porch and, inside, the round arches of the S aisle also remain from that early church. The remainder is mostly Perpendicular although blocked 13th century lancets remain. The North chapel is crowded with elaborate monuments and tomb-chests of members of the large North family. In his will, dated 1521, Richard Pytchye left money to pay for major refurbishment. The bowl of the font rests on top of a capital. A brass, dated 1553, remembers Edward Myrfin who travelled far in

Kirtling

his short life, to Greece, Armenia and Syria, but returned home to die at the age of 27.

KNAPWELL *All Saints* [D6]
Another secluded church lying well hidden from the road. The neatness of the flint and rubble exterior is the result of the restoration in 1866 by William Fawcett of Cambridge. The tower is one of a group of five in the county (Barton, Caldecote, Coton and Hatley St. George) which are thought to be the work of the same master mason, built within a forty-year period c.1400. The building fell into a ruinous state in the 18th century and the chancel collapsed. It was shortened and rebuilt in 1753. The decay continued until the Revd. Henry Brown revived its fortunes when he was appointed curate in 1861. The interior is largely Victorian with decorative red and black brickwork and apsed chancel. Notice the primitive faces on the font and the round-arched decoration on the stem. The Revd. W. V. Awdry, of *Thomas the Tank Engine* fame, was rector here 1946-55.

LANDBEACH *All Saints* [E6]
Alarming gargoyles greet you outside but the nave roof holds welcoming angels. Recently fragments of Norman masonry have been discovered, showing that a 12th century stone church once stood here. Jack Ravensdale details the church's history in his book *The Domesday Inheritance* and tells of tithes from All Saints being made over to the Augustinian canons at Barnwell in 1119. There is much fine woodwork: the Rood Screen; the pulpit with painted panels which came from Jesus College in 1787; medieval benches, one with the blacksmith's symbols; two 14th-century misericords in the choir stalls. The lovely roof may well have been built by Nicholas Toftys who lived in the village: it is known that he built the roof of St. Benet's in Cambridge in c.1450. A distinctly unusual angel carries the lectern on his back (perhaps 17th century Dutch craftsmanship). Traces of delicate vine-like painting remain behind the pulpit. The truly massive parish chest is early 14th century.

Landbeach

LANDWADE *St. Nicholas* [G6]
Delightful unspoilt country church, moated and surrounded by fields. Difficult to find but worth persevering (turn up Landwade Road then first right, it's hard to see as there is no welcoming spire). Built about 1445 for Sir Walter Cotton, and if you enjoy family histories you will enjoy reading the tablets and monuments recounting the lives and deaths of the Cotton family, Lords of the Manor here since the 15th century. One son died from a fall from his horse at Secunderabad, another in Colombo. In the N aisle you will find Sir John (d. 1593) and Dame Isabell and read of their 13 children; look at the details of the figures, her feet peeping out from beneath the many-layered petticoat. Admire also the delicate work of the faded 15th century Rood Screen and the medieval glass (c.1450) which has survived.

LEIGHTON BROMSWOLD *St. Mary* [B5]
The church is visible for miles around, standing as it does on the ridge that parallels the road between Huntingdon and Oundle. The massive square tower was rebuilt in c.1640, possibly designed by Inigo Jones. The church had been in a ruinous state when the poet

Leighton Bromswold

George Herbert (1593-1633) was appointed Prebend in 1626 and took on the task of rebuilding and furnishing it. Much of the interior dates to this period, including the roof which had collapsed. Herbert insisted on the identical pulpit and reader's desk, emphasizing the equal importance of preaching and prayer. The benches in the chancel are not choir stalls but seats for the celebration of communion, as the communion table then stood lengthwise in the centre of the chancel. The congregation went up into the chancel for the Holy Communion which followed Matins, for which they would have been in the nave. Light floods in through the large clear windows, though the dating of those in the chancel is difficult. Some are 15th century and others may be the result of the 17th century restoration, using an earlier style. The elaborate piscina remains from the Early English building, and is one of the best examples of this design. Similar piscinas are found elsewhere in the county, including Jesus College, Arrington, Burrough Green and Histon. After he died, George Herbert's poems were published by his friend Nicholas Ferrar, leader of the nearby community of Little Gidding.

LEVERINGTON St. Leonard [E1]

This handsome church dominates the surrounding Fenland. The lower part of the tower is Early English and the elegant spire rises above an embattled belfry and four octagonal turrets. The early 14th century porch is quite stunning, almost shrine-like and somewhat reminiscent of the Slipper Chapel near Walsingham. The chancel with triple sedilia is Early English, the S chapel a little later with the softer flowing lines of the Decorated period. Nave arcades and clerestory are Perpendicular. The late medieval colourful lectern is supported by six cheerful lions and the magnificent font has saints surrounding the bowl, angels below and more figures around the stem. The 15th century Jesse window in the N aisle was beautifully restored in 1900. Many memorials in the chapel, mostly to the Swaine family. Interesting headstones in the churchyard, one with a crowned head and weeping angels; another 1701-18 to Susanna Griplin and her children.

Leverington

LINTON St. Mary the Virgin [F8]

Tucked away from the busy main street and overlooked by lovely medieval buildings. The unusual round clerestory windows are the result of a late medieval heightening of an earlier Norman clerestory, some of which can still be seen. The church was largely rebuilt in the 14th century, though the four-arched S arcade remains as a good example of the Early English period. The N arcade is perhaps 100 years later, by which time the masons needed only a three-arched span. The tower was built about 1300. Splendid monument, signed by Wilton, to Elizabeth Bacon and her brother Peter Standly (1792). A ledger slab in the floor of the S chapel is badly defaced, dated perhaps 1538, and reads "Pray for the souls of ..." the remainder is illegible, doubtless erased during the period of the Commonwealth. Also read the small brasses of 20th century worshippers here.

LITLINGTON *St. Catherine* [D8]

Handsome long flint and rubble building with a low tower and flushwork decoration in the buttresses. The strongly carved Norman doorway in the chancel is blocked, and is almost all that remains of the 12th century church. A major rebuilding, including the clerestory, took place during the early 14th century, the Decorated period. The lovely font has elaborate but worn carving of angels and animals. Tall rood screen overlooked by extra windows either side of the chancel arch to throw more light on the rood itself. Fascinating graffiti in a S aisle window refer to Francis Drake's ambitious voyage in 1570; and in the N aisle near the organ is scratched in Latin "As on sea so on land" and signed by Robert Bownest 1594.

LITTLE ABINGTON *St. Mary* [F7]

Lovely situation looking across the fields to St. Mary's in Great Abington. Large stones in the E of the nave may well be reused from the Saxon church which once stood here. Both doorways have round Norman arches and the nave may be early 12th century, leading on to the 13th century building of the chancel. Major restoration by J. P. St. Aubyn in 1885 no doubt saved it all from total ruin. The chancel floor would have been raised at this time, which puts the Early English piscina, with its dogtooth decoration, in an awkwardly low position now. One window depicting the Adoration of the Magi is by Kempe (1901).

LITTLE CHISHILL *St. Nicholas* [E9]

Country churches are usually easy to find but you can easily drive past St. Nicholas as the tiled roof and low tower are almost hidden, tucked away in a very unspoiled part of the county. The S porch is decorated with shields and worn corbels; there is seating on either side and decorative strips of blank arcading beside the windows. A round-headed window remains from the Norman chancel but the piscina is from the 13th century building. Several memorials to members of the Crossman family; the reredos in memory of one brother who died in the Great War; the younger brother in World War II. The E window by Kempe and Tower (*c.*1916). Much of the remainder is in the Perpendicular style of the 15th century, including the rather nice N door with its worn quatrefoil decoration to the outside.

LITTLE EVERSDEN *St. Helen* [D7]

Simple country church with a lovely medieval timber porch. An earlier, steeper roofline can be seen on the E wall of the 15th century tower; walk round to the W wall of the tower and see the two quaint heads as corbels on the typical Perpendicular window. Inside, the walls are whitewashed, in stark contrast to the dark and stately choir stalls which came from Queens' College, Patron here since 1549. Dedications to St. Helen are unusual in the county; only Colne, Folksworth and Bourne are dedicated to the mother of the Emperor Constantine who was converted to Christianity at the same time as her son, in 312.

LITTLE GIDDING *St. John the Evangelist* [B4]

It is so unexpected compared with the large medieval churches with their grand spires in the neighbouring villages; the community at Little Gidding worships in what at first sight appears to be a rather plain diminutive

Little Gidding

Little Gransden

the *Four Quartets*. In 1977 community life began here once more and flourishes today. Visitors are always welcome in the Parlour in the main farmhouse.

Little Gidding

brick building. Nicholas Ferrar installed the panelling in 1626, but it was extensively restored in 1714. The brass tablets behind the altar, the lectern and the unique brass font were all put here by Ferrar; the lid of the font is still twisted as a result of being thrown in the nearby pond during the raid of 1646. Nicholas Ferrar died in 1637 but the community continued until the death of his brother 20 years later. It was not until the late 1930s that interest was again shown in the importance of the Ferrar Community, and T. S. Eliot wrote "Little Gidding", the last of

LITTLE GRANSDEN *St. Peter and St. Paul* [C7]
Less imposing than its neighbour at Great Gransden, and the exterior is largely the result of extensive restorations by the Victorians. The tower is 15th century and much of the interior 13th century. The medieval screen has been restored and repainted, but one or two strange worn heads survive: a small face, perhaps a Green Man, and what looks like a benign hippopotamus; a sheaf of wheat and a bunch of grapes too, symbolizing the bread and wine. Some wall-paintings survive over the chancel arch. Beside the W door a graffito shows a man with a sword, but he is upside down - a deliberate mistake when reusing stone, or a medieval workman in a hurry?

LITTLE PAXTON *St. James* [B6]
The tympanum, over the S doorway, is Norman, and shows Christ the Good Shepherd with the lamb, to the left of the Cross, and to the right is what may be a wolf pursuing a lamb. Another reminder of the 12th century is the top of a round-headed window in the S wall of the chancel. In the nave, notice the tower buttresses are inside the church, so the tower was built before the nave itself. Beside a window in the chancel S wall, you can see

some remarkable medieval graffiti - especially that of a horse which looks remarkably like a fine example of our Suffolk Punch horse today. Originally this church may have been a Chapel of Ease to the Minster church of Great Paxton so that the priests would then have had to ferry between the two.

LITTLEPORT St. George [F4]

Mainly 15th century with a fine tower which once had a passageway through its base, probably because it was built to the edge of the churchyard. A second nave and N aisle were added in 1857 and have

Little Paxton

recently been converted into parish rooms. The retable and stone reredos are 19th century as is much of the stained glass. Soft colours in the E window, by Geoffrey Webb (look for his spiderweb mark); another, the scene at Emmaus, is by Martin Travers, using stronger colours. In S aisle a window dated 1953 has little illustrations of life here in the Fen country. Nearby is an enormous ironbound chest dated 1672. Outside the chancel E window is an early headstone (1794), showing a weeping figure seated by a tree.

LITTLEPORT St. Matthew [F4]

A small Victorian church built in the fen in 1879, away from the town. The attractive and well proportioned Rood Screen has been moved to the W end of the nave where it now frames the font. The First World War memorial has many names on it from this small community. Small side chapels to N and S are cherished by the parishioners.

LITTLE SHELFORD All Saints [E7]

The Norman doorway and the N and S chancel walls remain from the 12th century building. However, a double-splayed window high up in the S wall of the chancel is pre-Conquest and the interlace pattern panels may be reused from a 10th century building. The church is filled with memorials to members of the de Freville family. Sir John (d. 1312) may have been responsible for the rebuilding and his effigy lies under an elaborate canopy in the chancel. Panelling (c.1450) is brightly painted with the de Freville arms. 17th century pulpit with sounding board; de Freville brasses in the chancel floor. The fine 15th century chantry chapel has two charming brasses, the couples holding hands and watched by three little dogs, symbols of loyalty. The two alabaster statues were found beneath the chancel floor in 1854.

LITTLE STUKELY St. Martin [C5]

The church was thoroughly restored during the 19th century by Robert Hutchinson, who went to great lengths to preserve parts of the 12th century building. Norman column-shafts are set into the S wall of the tower; more fragments are displayed inside the tower and on the S arch of the N chapel. Much carving of corbels survives and a large winged man is the first to catch the eye. On the SE pier notice the scene of an unfortunate individual being devoured by a monster, now used to support the hymn numbers. The Old Hundredth is written high in the S aisle and it looks as if the painter was working on an unsteady ladder and also without any guide lines to help him. A fine small brass of William Halls in clerical dress (1617).

LITTLE THETFORD St. George [F5]

Small, low and attractive with all the details of a 14th century church when seen from the outside. Attractive flat-headed Decorated windows in nave. The W end of the nave is now used regularly for various village groups. The medieval font on an octagonal stem still retains a little of its original colour and worn carved heads on the four panels.

LITTLE WILBRAHAM *St. John* [F7]

A large Saxon cemetery was found close by but if there was a Saxon church here, nothing remains of it now; the chancel and nave are both 13th century. A tiny Norman round-headed window survives in the S aisle looking out on to the huge base of the churchyard cross. Rather lovely 15th century S door with shields of the Burgh, Lisle(2) and Bourchier families. Major restoration was carried out about 1850 including renewal of the roofs; three of the original medieval figures have been retained. There is a large squint N of the chancel arch but it no longer has a view of the High Altar. In the chancel floor a fine brass of William Blakway (d.1521). The 14th century tower is certainly unusual with almost-flying buttresses supporting the arch; outside from the W notice its large base, with tapering later stages. Recent repair work has unveiled a large flintwork cross in the N outer wall of the N aisle. It resembles a Maltese Cross and the Revd. Brian Kerley suggests that, bearing in mind the dedication of the church, it may be connected with the Knights of St. John; or perhaps it may be a Bishop's dedication cross for the massive N aisle.

LODE *St. James* [F6]

A carefully tended churchyard and a path of yew trees leads to this attractive Victorian church designed by Rhode Hawkins. No tower, but a little bell-cote and a welcoming timber porch. The clock, by Dent of London, was installed when the church was completed in 1853. A beautiful Italian 18th century silk embroidered altar frontal. The Lady Chapel was built by the Fairhaven family in 1960-62 and the memorial here to Lord Fairhaven (1966) reads "lover of all things beautiful."

Lode

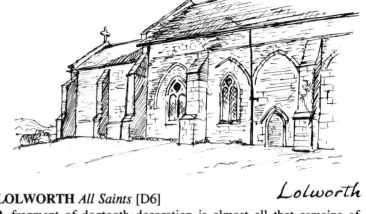

Lolworth

LOLWORTH *All Saints* [D6]

A fragment of dogtooth decoration is almost all that remains of the 13th century church. A small piece of frieze shows the ballflower ornament used during the Decorated period of the early 14th century; Pevsner compares this fragment with that seen at St. Mary's, Over. In 1393 Thomas of Walsingham recorded that "lightenings and thunders did much damage" and caused most of the village and the church to be burned; the field adjacent to the church is still known as Burnt Close. All Saints was rebuilt without aisles, though the blocked arcades can still be seen, and it was rededicated in 1406. The 14th century font has survived and beside it is the base of the medieval churchyard cross. The 16th century panel painting in the chancel, showing the Raising of Lazarus, was found in a ruined Belgian church during the Great War. The Rood and Stations of the Cross were given to All Saints by Revd. E. J. Dredge, rector here from 1926-31.

LONGSTANTON *All Saints* [D6]

Built largely in the Decorated style; the tracery in the windows of the S transept is a joyful example of the period. The ogee arch of the early 14th century is used over the triple sedilia in the chancel; but a small N window must have been in the earlier chancel. There were low-side windows to the N and S; both are blocked now but they retain the iron grating. In the N aisle is a handsomely carved 16th century family pew. The S transept contains many memorials to the Hatton family, Lords of the

Manor since the days of Elizabeth I. Sir Francis Drake's ship *The Golden Hind* was named in honour of the crest of his patron Sir Christopher Hatton. An elaborate monument to Sir Thomas Hatton (d. 1658) shows Sir Thomas and Lady Hatton; her hand is in a partly open purse, perhaps as a mark of her generous nature. Heraldic glass here also as Hatton memorials. Do make a point of looking at the Perpendicular font: its eight panels are carved as a sampler of the different styles of window tracery of the period. The tower and S porch are a little later, in the Perpendicular style.

LONGSTANTON *St. Michael* [D6]

Not far from the parish church of All Saints is this lovely little 13th century building. Carefully restored in 1884, it is a rare and unspoiled church built in 1286. It retains its thatched roof on nave and aisles and a simple interior, except for the elaborate double piscina, similar to those at Jesus College in Cambridge, Histon, Arrington and Caxton. The well under the large chestnut tree was used for baptisms for centuries; tradition has it that the sun must shine through the open cross in the brickwork before the mark could

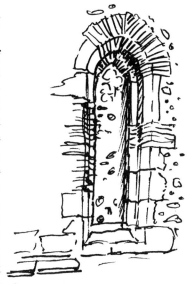

Longstanton-St Michael

Longstanton-St Michael

be made on the baby's head. (It may have been restored incorrectly, as it doesn't seem possible the way it is now.) St. Michael's is now in the care of the Redundant Churches Fund.

LONGSTOWE *St. Mary the Virgin* [D7]

A very attractive church now; but like many others it fell into great disrepair and the medieval tower was used as a dovecote during the 18th century. It now stands comfortably beside the Victorian nave and chancel, rebuilt by William Fawcett of Cambridge in 1864. In the N chapel two remarkable monuments crowd into each other. Below lies Anthony Cage, with his 6 sons and 4 daughters. He was the builder of Longstowe Hall and died in 1603. The effigy beside him may be from another tomb, as the style of the lady does not correspond with that of the baronet. William Cole, the 18th century historian, saw the original Cage tomb when it was in the chancel. It was so enormous that the altar was off-centre and the Bishop unsuccessfully demanded its removal. Sir Anthony now gazes up at the remarkable allegorical memorial to Sir Ralph Bovey (d. 1679). A lovely sculpture by Hans Feibusch is a memorial to Temple Bevan (d. 1981); it shows St. Michael carrying the soul to heaven. A 14th century bell hangs in the tower.

LONGTHORPE (Peterborough) *St. Botolph* [B3]

Dedicated to the patron saint of wayfarers. This lovely, simple, 13th century church is one of the oldest buildings in Peterborough. Permission to rebuild was given in 1263-4 by the Abbot of Peterborough to Sir William de Thorpe and the tall narrow lancets are typical of the period. The interior is noteworthy for 20th century craftsmanship; much of the handsome woodwork was given as memorials during and after the Great War, including the reredos, the rood and the communion rail. A window in the N aisle commemorates a Parish warden who spent "40 happy years" here. Statues beside the altar are of St. Botolph, holding the church, and Peada, the founder of the Abbey at Peterborough in 654.

Madingley

MADINGLEY *St. Mary Magdalene* [D6]

The church stands at the entrance to Madingley Hall. The medieval village which once surrounded the church was moved out of sight of the Hall, as a result of extensive reshaping of the landscape in the 18th century. The 12th century bowl of the font may be the oldest visible remains of an earlier church; the base on which it stands is later. A lancet window remains from the Early English period; the chancel, nave and elegant tower arch are mainly 14th century Decorated. Bishop Alcock, Comptroller of the King's Works to Henry VIII, is remembered by his rebus here as a corbel. Lovely 17th century Communion Rail originally from Great St. Mary's in Cambridge. Sir John Cotton, Lord of the Manor, spent £300 rebuilding the chancel in 1770-80, shortening it by 12 feet and re-setting the E window. Interesting monuments: Jane Hinde (1692), reclining on a cushion; an anchor memorial to Sir Charles Cotton, Admiral of the White (d. 1812), by Flaxman; and Mrs. Jane Cotton, kneeling and partly hidden at the W of the N aisle (d. 1707). Edward VII stayed at the Hall during his student days and his Coat of Arms hangs inside the church.

MANEA *St. Nicholas* [E4]

Completely rebuilt in 1875, by Peter Ruddle of Peterborough. Some interesting interior brickwork, especially the false arcading in the nave. 19th century glass in the E window. Much evidence throughout of the Victorian stonemason: notice the font and lectern, also the angel corbels in the chancel. A 17th century altar remains from the earlier church.

Madingley

MARCH *St. John the Evangelist* Station Road [E3]

Designed by T. H. Wyatt in 1871 when the population of March was expanding with the building of the railway. Rock-faced exterior with bellcote and tiny spire. Victorian glass throughout.

MARCH *St. Mary* Westry [E3]

An attractive church designed by T. H. Wyatt in 1873. It serves a large rural area and stands surrounded by a large open churchyard on the Wisbech Road about a mile from the town. The bellcote is topped with a small tower. There is a prettily painted pulpit and, in the porch, a small stained glass window of "The Sower."

MARCH *St. Peter* High Street [E3]
A large rock-faced building on the High Street. Designed in 1880 by T. H. Wyatt, the architect for two other churches built in March during the previous decade. Here there is a large broach spire rising between four turrets. Wide arcades and all generally in the Early English style.

MARCH *St. Wendreda* High Street [E3]
Above all, allow yourself time here to admire the astonishing "angel roof" of *c.*1500, more correctly known as a double hammerbeam roof. If the light is bright enough, you can distinguish some of the figures: to the N Christ with hand raised in blessing, opposite St. Matthew holding a globe. The excellent guide booklet explains it all. The building is in the Decorated and Perpendicular styles, except for the chancel which was rebuilt in 1872. A passage through the base of the tower was necessary as it was built over a public right of way. A papal indulgence was granted in 1343 to those donating towards the cost of the "new building." The remains of St. Wendreda were returned here the same year. Towards the end of the 15th century another costly building period included the porch, chancel arch, clerestory with flint and flushwork, quatrefoil friezes and battlements, and of course the "angel roof." Happily the roof was spared by the commissioners of Edward VI, when they visited March in 1546. They may have considered the roof to be too recent to justify its destruction. It is recorded that they were well wined and dined when they visited the town. Good 16th century brasses also survive, possibly of important donors towards the rebuilding campaigns.

MARHOLM *St. Mary* [B2]
Lovely rural setting and sheltered by majestic cedars. The low tower is Norman, and arcades and chancel arch remain from a major rebuilding towards the end of the 13th century. Usually the tower dominates the outline of a church but here the tower is only

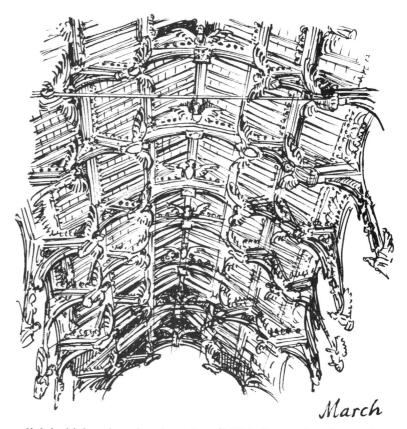

March

slightly higher than the chancel roof. This impressive chancel is the result of ambitious rebuilding by Sir William Fitzwilliam of Milton. He died in 1534 and expressed a wish that he should be buried in the chancel "lately edified" by him. Splendid monuments here to several generations of his family, many of which have been recently restored. Another Sir William died in Ireland in 1599 "worn out by the fatigues of the war and state there"; he lies now holding hands with his wife Anne. Read the inscription on Edward Hunter's memorial (d. 1646). There are many more. In the S aisle the fine effigy on the altar tomb is thought to be that of Sir John de Wittelbury, Lord of the Manor of Marholm at the end of the 14th century. Interesting heraldic glass of the Fitzwilliam family. An unusual font, quite plain except for two large roses.

MAXEY *St. Peter* [B2]

The church now stands isolated from the village. Originally it stood equidistant from the three parishes it served; two have long vanished and Maxey was the only one to flourish. The substantial Norman tower was probably built by the master mason responsible for that at nearby Castor. The 12th century church here was large; both aisles date from the Norman period and the small round windows of that clerestory can be seen from inside the nave. In the tower arch two Green Men, their faces surrounded by foliage, gaze down from the tower arch. The Lady Chapel (*c.*1367) is separated from the N aisle by an elegant archway; nearby a shelf is supported by a grinning, whistling face. A magnificent rood screen and loft once graced the chancel arch. It was donated by Margaret of Lancaster, the mother of Henry VII. The loft was large enough to hold an altar and the piscina can still be seen high on the S wall, a very rare feature. (Another can be seen at St. Peter, Horningsea, near Cambridge.)

MELBOURN *All Saints* [D8]

A handsome building of flint and rubble, with flushwork decoration around the base on the south and west walls only; an economy found necessary in many churches. Parts of the 13th century building remain, including the lancets in the chancel and the double piscina. A little later, about 1300, came the Decorated style typified by the ogee arch, found here above the priest's door in the chancel. About 1500 a major rebuilding took place when the style now known as Perpendicular came into fashion. Most of the windows, which make this interior so light, date from this time; the tower was also rebuilt and the decorative bases added. Two members of the Hitch family bequeathed money towards the cost of the elegant rood screen: Robert (d. 1504) and Thomas (d. 1508). The marvellous nave roof can also be dated by the rebus (a cockerel) of Bishop Alcock of Ely.

MELDRETH *Holy Trinity* [D8]

There is much to admire. The tower is late 12th century, the transitional period between the Norman and Early English. A walk round to the N reveals three elegant Decorated windows of

Meldreth

the early 14th century; also a small late 12th century doorway. Inside, remains of extensive wall-paintings can be seen. Medieval pulpit and rood screen. The earliest part is the chancel with 2 round headed Norman windows; the E window is a 19th century addition. The splendid "finger and barrel" organ was bought from Bassingbourn in 1866 for £100; it is thought to be the only working model in the county.

MEPAL *St. Mary* [E4]

A lovely little church surrounded by fields. Although it was heavily restored three times between 1849 and 1905, the lancet windows remain in the chancel and tower from the 13th century building. The simple Early English piscina is from the same period. There is a round-headed low side window in S chancel wall. Small 14th century niches under ogee arches on either side of the E window. A memorial tells of the interesting life of James Fortra, a refugee from Brabant, who became a courtier.

MILTON *All Saints* [E6]

Turn beside the Jolly Brewer and you will find the medieval church tucked away beside the new Children's Hospice. The Saxons built a timber church here but the oldest part of All Saints must be the solid Norman chancel arch. A major restoration was carried out in 1864 and the chancel was largely rebuilt, including the E window. The Communion Rail came from King's College Chapel in the 17th century. Interesting brass (1553) in the chancel to "the great Judge Coke". Also a fine marble monument to Mrs. Knight (d. 1800) by Flaxman. More recently a modern extension has been added to the north. Outside the chancel E wall a tablet placed by "his Master and Mistress for his faithful service" recalls Thomas Cannon who died in 1726.

MOLESWORTH *St. Peter* [A5]

The steep chancel roof dominates the flat aisleless nave, similar to that at nearby Brington. The chancel was rebuilt in 1884 and the blank arcading around the windows and the large chancel arch were put in, following the original Early English style. 16th century wall-paintings with St. Christopher on the N wall; opposite can just be seen St. Anthony and his pig. The E window was given by the widow of the Revd. Henry Penzer (d. 1929); he is shown kneeling in a purple cassock and in the lower windows are shown his churches at Molesworth and Keyston. A hundred or so yards away from St. Peter's churchyard, on private land, is a Pets' Cemetery where all manner of animals were buried in the early part of this century; little headstones remember "Dear Bobbie - Jim's Chum" (1909) and "Dear Jumbo" (1910).

MORBORNE *All Saints* [B3]

An early 17th century brick tower stands happily beside the medieval nave and chancel. The Norman chancel arch has been dated about 1140, followed by the N arcade about 1240 and the S arcade later still. Three small recesses above the 13th century double piscina were perhaps to hold the communion vessels. A wall-painting can just be seen in the N window in the chancel. The early 13th century effigy in the S aisle may be the Abbot responsible for bulding All Saints; his feet rest on two human heads. The square font now lying in the S aisle looks even earlier than the 12th century font now in use.

MURROW *Corpus Christi* [D2]

A simple red brick church built in 1857 in the Early English style. A brightly painted chancel, shining pews and the lovely little 19th century organ are all lovingly cared for. Very elegant 18th century font.

NEWBOROUGH *St. Bartholomew* [C2]

A small brick church built in the mid-19th century to serve the needs of the newly established community in the Fens. There are Commandment Boards beside the entrance to the chancel and a very attractive E window by A. K. Nicholson dated 1938.

NEWTON Nr. Cambridge *St. Margaret* [E8]

The earlier church was cruciform, i.e. with transepts north and south. A 13th century lancet, a piscina and a fragment of a wall-painting remain in the S transept. About 100 years later aisles were needed as the congregation grew, and the transept roofs were raised. The tower is late 14th century. Dowsing visited here in 1644 on his voyage of destruction. William Cole wrote in 1742 that the chancel was "new". Some very good monuments; many of them memorials to the Pemberton family. Christopher, an early war journalist, died at the Battle of Sedan in 1870. An unusual Art Nouveau memorial (1900). There is a massive 13th century font which Norman Scarfe compares to the very similar example at Shepreth. In the churchyard the Poynter mausoleum, 1922, is a memorial to the Walston family.

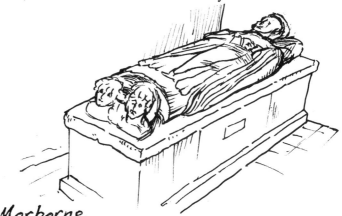

Morborne

NEWTON-IN-THE-ISLE
St. James [E1]

St. James is the patron saint of pilgrims, but the original dedication here was to St. Catherine. Stout round piers in the nave remain from the Norman building; the arcades were raised during the 1300s, perhaps at the same time as the tower was built. The clerestory and Perpendicular windows of the chancel are a century later. In 1879 a major restoration was necessary; a vestry was added and bells and belfry repaired. The rood screen is a late 19th century replacement; notice the unusal embattled walkway at the top of the medieval rood stairs. A large font with blank shields. Window in N aisle is signed by Easton, 1931, using his distinctive symbol. Interesting headstones in the churchyard.

Newton-in-the-Isle

NORTHBOROUGH St. Andrew [B2]

A very interesting place to visit, although it does give a first impression that the builders left abruptly without completing their task. The ambitious building, S of the chancel, of the elaborate Delamare chantry chapel, designed to be part of a greatly enlarged church, was never completed, and this small parish had not the means to do so. The exuberant craftsmanship in the lavish Decorated style is much in evidence; the ballflower frieze and flowing window tracery is all typical of the early 14th century

mason. Compare the quite plain W end of the church and belfry which remain from the much simpler 12th century building. Fragments of wall-paintings in nave and S aisle. Oliver Cromwell's widow, Elizabeth, is buried here.

OAKINGTON St. Andrew [E6]

Very attractive church with uniform Perpendicular windows on the N side; part of a much earlier window can be seen in W wall of S aisle. The tower was built about 1300, and on the E wall is the outline of a steeper nave roof. The lancets in the chancel, and both arcades, are part of the Early English building. The medieval screen no longer stands in the chancel arch but parts of the dado remain in the N aisle. Attractive 15th century niches either side of the Perpendicular window in N aisle. Much rebuilding was necessary during the 19th century. Close to the font is a simply carved stand for the Visitors' Book, given by members of 7 Squadron RAF, one of the valiant Pathfinder squadrons of World War II. Outside, parts of the older building have been reused in the S aisle. On a sundial are carved the words "God always cares."

OFFORD CLUNY All Saints [C6]

The Abbots of Cluny in Burgundy were Lords of the Manor here until the 15th century. The arcades and chancel arch remain from the Early English 13th century building. The Perpendicular embattled tower has three quatrefoil windows. A plain Early English doorway remains in the N wall. The short brick chancel was built in 1726; a faint outline of the earlier chancel roof can just be seen. Look up to admire the silent congregation here: six large figures in this medieval "angelic roof", their hair bound by cross and diadem. Pulpit is Elizabethan, the lectern Jacobean. The medieval font was found in pieces about 70 years ago; it now holds flowers in the churchyard.

OFFORD DARCY St. Peter [C6]

Standing all too close to the railway line and no longer in regular use; but it is worth finding the key to see the simple interior. Lovely ballflower frieze around the top of the S nave wall, typical of the Decorated period of the early 14th century. Inside, the N arcade is Norman; the chancel is later, i.e. Early English. Notice the unusual angle piscina in the S arcade. The rood screen is also of the Decorated period; few such early screens survive. Interesting early 15th century brasses and several monuments here. Notice the one to Richard Nailour (d.1616) surrounded here by his two wives, two sons and six daughters. The church is now in the care of the Redundant Churches Fund.

Old Hurst

OLD HURST *St. Peter* [D5]

A lovely little church and an unspoiled example of the Early English period, as you see from the lancet windows and the pointed arch of the S doorway. No tower, just a double bellcote. The font is of the same period. An unusual pillar piscina, in a corner of the chancel, is perhaps Norman and therefore earlier still. The stone altar slab has also survived. Outside, notice the weathered faces on corbels on S wall. A tablet on the E wall marks its rebuilding in 1903.

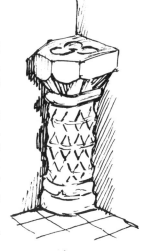

Old Hurst

OLD WESTON *St. Swithin* [A5]

Now almost isolated though until the 1840s there were many houses around the church. The porch has a string-course matching that of the tower; perhaps the porch which may have had an upper room, was moved when the S aisle was added. The N door may be as early as 1200 and outside has rough nailhead decoration. The chancel is late 13th century and the finer nailhead decoration on some of the arcades indicates these were completed about the same time. In 1895 a series of wall-paintings were discovered, three layers deep in some places. The dedication is unique in Cambridgeshire although there are 58 other churches in the country dedicated to St. Swithin. His relics were translated into Winchester cathedral on July 15th 971, when miraculous cures occurred and heavy rains fell, as further testament to his powers. His shrine at Winchester became a famous pilgrimage centre until it was destroyed at the Reformation; it was restored in 1962.

ORTON LONGUEVILLE *Holy Trinity* [B3]

Lovely tracery on the E window greets the visitor. A handsome church with battlements on tower and chancel. The building dates largely from 1280-1300; the flowery hinges on the priest's door are thought to be *c.*1320. A quatrefoil window remains in the Decorated porch, restored in 1675. The chancel is mainly Decorated and the ogee form is used as well as some ballflower ornament. Strangely, a small blocked lancet frame is set low on the N wall; shallow niches with seats either side of the arch. Interesting monuments especially in N chapel; notice also the memorial in the S aisle to Sir Charles Cope (d.1781).

ORTON WATERVILLE *St. Mary* [B3]

Attractive 13th century stone porch and S doorway. Inside, notice the good example of 'stiff leaf' decoration on one of the capitals in the S arcade. Early 14th century, Decorated, windows in both aisles but the more simple lines of the chancel windows are 17th century. The Elizabethan pulpit is extravagantly carved and is said to have come from Great St. Mary's in Cambridge. The royal arms of the Stuarts are finely carved and hang over the tower

He had been tutor to the young Richard II, but was impeached and beheaded in 1388. The wonderful roof was reconstructed by an 18th century Rector here and the colours restored again in 1883. Late medieval choir stalls, many with misericords, may have come from Trinity College. Interesting memorials to several Masters. The clock (*c*.1616) is perhaps the oldest working public clock in the country; this also came from Trinity College in *c*.1740. In the S aisle is a mutilated but still exquisite statue of the crucifixion; carved in the early 14th century, it was hidden away to escape the excesses of the Reformation and only discovered in the 19th century. Unusual Royal Arms (1686) for King James II.

Orton Waterville

Orwell

Orwell

doorway. 15th century pinnacles once topped the tower, but were taken down in 1929 and still lie forlornly on the grass.

ORWELL *St. Andrew* [D7]
This lovely church stands high above the road and holds much of interest. In the porch notice the fragment of Saxon carving with the interlace design; another carving dates from the 12th century. Most of the interior is 14th century. The magnificent chancel, in the early Perpendicular style, was built in 1398 by the Rector as a memorial to the Lord of the Manor.

OVER *St. Mary* [D5]

Before you enter, walk around to the N and notice the quite grand aisle built in the early 14th century. The large Decorated windows are impressive, and the ballflower ornament completes the lavish appearance. On the W face of the tower is a deteriorating medieval carving of the Assumption of the Virgin Mary. To the S and see more ballflower decoration and the splendid porch still in the Decorated style. Wonderful gargoyles: an owl, and many grotesque faces; the lion and water-bearer to the E of the porch perhaps had some astrological significance. Inside there are carvings everywhere; little faces around all the capitals including one head with three faces, rather like a Toby Jug. The choir stalls on the S wall of the chancel came from Ramsey Abbey and the 3 rams' heads can be seen on one of the misericords. Fine Jacobean pulpit; tucked away underneath are heads representing the seven deadly sins. The medieval screen retains its coving on the chancel side only. Some very decorative wall-painting in the S aisle. The spire and tower were badly damaged in the 1987 hurricane.

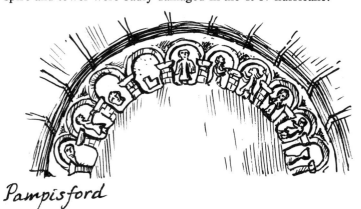

Pampisford

PAMPISFORD *St. John* [E8]

Described by William Cole, the antiquary, in 1742, as "a very neat pile of building". The W wall of the tower shows the three stages of its building beginning in the early 14th century. The S doorway is much older and above it is a remarkable Norman tympanum, detailing, from right to left, the life of John the Baptist. It includes a font symbolizing the baptism; Salome; John, winged as an angel; the severed head. The building is largely 13th century but much restoration was carried out in the 19th century, under the direction of Revd. Brocklebank. The vestry was added, nave roof renewed, a family pew added with curved front to allow access to the vestry. Windows are filled with Victorian glass, some by Kempe. A window in S aisle (1982) recalls Brytnoth, Earl of Northampton, a Saxon noble who led the English forces against the Danes and died in 990 at the Battle of Maldon. In 1978 a new peal of six bells was installed.

PAPWORTH EVERARD *St. Peter* [C6]

Rebuilt in the 19th century after it had fallen into a ruinous state. The tale of destruction was helped no doubt by a visit from the infamous William Dowsing, the zealous Parliamentary Visitor in East Anglia (*c.*1640). He carried out his instructions to destroy all adornment and icons with considerable success and here he recorded the defacing of wall-paintings and statues of the four evangelists. The tower was demolished later by the hurricane of 1741, which caused a huge amount of damage in the area. A new tower was not built until 1870. The church enjoys happier times now and all is lovingly cared for.

PAPWORTH St. AGNES *St. John the Baptist* [C6]

The church is covered with attractive chequerwork and is a fine example of a 19th century rebuilding. Only the tower arch remains from another major restoration in 1530, initiated by Anthony Mallory. Notice the lions' faces on the downpipes and guttering. Declared redundant in 1976 and only narrowly escaped demolition; but thanks to much determination by the villagers, it is in use once more and in the care of the Friends of Friendless Churches.

PARSON DROVE *Emmanuel* [D2]

Created out of the large Leverington parish in 1870, at the same time as Gorefield and Southea with Murrow. Built in 1872, by the Ecclesiastical Commissioners, in the Early English style. An apsed chancel. Red brickwork throughout with bands of black. No tower but a bellcote between nave and chancel.

Parson Drove

PARSON DROVE *St. John* [D2]

The Redundant Churches Fund has carefully restored this lovely building. The 15th century Perpendicular tower has a vaulted roof and impressive tower arch. The interior is light and spacious, thanks to all the plain glass and large clerestory windows. No chancel; it was washed away in a flood in 1613. A late 16th century communion table, with bulbous legs, stands under the 15th century window in the S aisle. The N aisle is older and has a curious shallow 13th century porch. The large font has elaborate decoration on bowl and stem.

PASTON *All Saints* [B2]

There is still a village-like feeling about the church despite its urban situation. The tower (*c.*1300) has a massive though narrow arch supported by two large crouching figures, perhaps monk and nun. The chantry chapel to the N of the chancel is earlier still. The low side window in the chancel is blocked now, but you can see where the hinges once hung and part of the catch remains. The medieval rood screen was removed during the last century and when it was replaced the lovely carvings at the top were mistakenly made to face away from the congregation. In the S aisle are fragments of sculpture with round Norman arches, possibly part of an elaborate reredos of an earlier church.

PEAKIRK *St. Pega* [B2]

Peakirk

Dedicated to Pega, a hermit at "Pega's kirk" or church, who died in 719. Pega's brother was St. Guthlac, one of England's most popular pre-Conquest hermit saints, who founded nearby Crowland Abbey in Lincolnshire. Much of St. Pega's church remains as it was in Norman times: the lovely S doorway, W wall and bellcote. The N arcade with round piers and arches is 12th century, the S arcade a century later. Important 14th century wall-paintings include the Quick and the Dead (with gruesome corpses and insects) and a Warning to Gossips (two women with a devil between them). The rare 14th century lectern stands on a slender eight-shafted stem with original stone base. The E window (1913) is by Kempe and recalls the 59 years of service by the rector here.

PETERBOROUGH *All Saints* Park Road [B3]

The foundation stone was laid on All Saints' Day, 1886. The architect was Temple Moore. Exactly one year later, the first service of worship was held in this handsome, Decorated style, church. Canon Richard Ball, having been 17 years at St. Paul's in Peterborough, then came to All Saints and remained for 20 years. He and his family were responsible for much of the furnishings in the new church. The oak lectern was given in memory of Canon Ball and also designed by Temple Moore, as is much of the carving here. A panel with a 15th century Della Robbia design hangs near the font.

PETERBOROUGH *St. Barnabas* Taverners Road [B3]
Built in 1900, by W. Bryer. A large brick building with some chequerboard decoration. Built as a daughter church of St. Mark's necessitated by the expansion of this area of the city. The church is now shared with the New Testament Church of God and the two congregations join for several services throughout the year.

PETERBOROUGH *Christ the Carpenter* Central Avenue [B3]
An unusual dedication for an Anglican church. The exterior is typical of the 1950s (the building was consecrated in July, 1958). The interior has warmth and sparkle. It has been called the poor man's Coventry Cathedral because of its distinctive shape and the orientation of the windows. The stained glass was added in the 1970s. Over the entrance is etched glass representing the Carpenter's tools. The statue of the Resurrection is by Oliffe Richmond, a pupil of Henry Moore.

PETERBOROUGH *St. John the Baptist* Cathedral Square [B3]
This very fine Perpendicular church was dedicated in 1407. It replaced an earlier 11th century building and much of the material was reused. Lovely S porch with vaulted ceiling and carved bosses of the Trinity, Annunciation and Crucifixion. The interior is light and spacious with tall, slender 15th century arcades. The large octagonal font has typical Perpendicular quatrefoil panels. Several good monuments, one by John Flaxman, 1826. Much restoration took place in the 1880s and the E window was inserted then. N aisle window by Kempe. Most of the woodwork is 20th century, including the rood screen and group.

Peterborough
-St Jude

PETERBOROUGH *St. Jude* Atherstone Avenue [B3]
Consecrated in July 1984, St. Jude has a dignity and warmth not always found in contemporary churches. The remarkable belltower may have been inspired by continental examples and holds three bells and a bat box. In the early 1960s a RAF hut was the only place for worship here, and a modest church hall was

built in 1968. The church now standing here was designed by 'Jo' Robotham and built by local craftsmen. It has acquired many interesting treasures in its short existence: the statue of St. Peter from Vèzelay in Burgundy; the rood group from a church in Teddington; the terracotta Stations of the Cross are the work of the Community of Little Sisters of Jesus at Walsingham and the statue of St. Jude was sculpted by Mother Concordia of Minster Abbey in Kent; the doorway and font are from the now demolished church at Benwick. There is also a peaceful walled garden.

PETERBOROUGH *St. Mark* Lincoln Road [B3]
Designed in 1856 by E. Ellis, when the arrival of the railway stimulated major expansion in the area. In fact St. Mark's was the first new church in the city since St. John's was rebuilt over 400 years before. The Victorians chose to use an early Decorated style. The tower is sited on the NE corner where it can best be seen from the road. The balustrading under the clerestory is unusual and the dormer windows (definitely not early Decorated) were added in 1906.

PETERBOROUGH *St. Paul* Lincoln Road, New England [B3]
Designed in 1868 by James Teale using the Early English style. Built to serve the "new" Great Northern Railway settlement. Impressive interior with sturdy apsed chancel. Tall lancets of the central tower lighten the unpainted rood figures and screen. The Stations of the Cross are beautifully crafted. The font is certainly quite ancient, but not even the 92 year old parishioner knew from whence it came.

PIDLEY *All Saints* [D5]
Attractive setting at the N end of the village. Rebuilt by William Fawcett, the Cambridge architect, in 1864. A drawing of the earlier church can be seen in the tower. The lovely old-fashioned churchyard has large lilac trees and headstones leaning in every direction. A particularly lovely early 18th century headstone under the E window.

PONDERSBRIDGE *St. Thomas* [C3]
Spacious Victorian church which replaced an earlier chapel nearby. In the early 1970s it was in such poor repair that it was closed for three years; but the efforts of a very small but loyal congregation raised enough money for the necessary rebuilding to be carried out. The acoustics are particularly good and it is regularly used for concerts as well as a place of worship.

Prickwillow

PRICKWILLOW *St. Peter* [F4]
The exquisite white marble font, with cherubs, pearls and shells, is reason enough to come here. It was given to Ely Cathedral in 1697 and has been here on loan for a hundred years. The church was built by Richard Rowe, the Cambridge architect and engineer in 1868. Stained glass by Heaton. Rev. Kingdon was rector here for 30 years until the end of World War I. The unusual shingled spire is a local landmark.

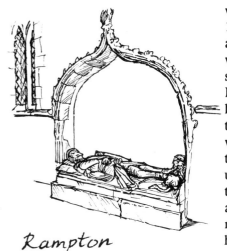

Rampton

was rebuilt during the early 14th century, when the ogee arch of the Decorated period was extensively used, and is seen here in a recess in the N wall. Very unusually the low-side window still has the original grille and wooden shutters; it may be that these windows were used to provide fresh air for the smoke-filled interiors, and were not used for ringing the sanctus bell or hearing confessions. The pulpit is Elizabethan and in the 18th century the brick S porch was added and the Communion Rail acquired.

Rampton

RAMPTON *All Saints* [E6]
There is a real feeling of peace and age about All Saints. The thatched roof is uncommon in Cambridgeshire and the medieval wall-paintings inside remind us of how colourful our churches once were. Most building periods are evident: fragments from Saxon coffin lids; a blocked Norman window and the jambs of the chancel arch are exceptionally wide apart for a 12th century village church; tower and S arcade Early English. The chancel

RAMSEY *St. Thomas of Canterbury* [C4]
Perhaps the finest Norman building in the county. Building began *c*.1190 and proceeded from E to W. It was intended as a hospital or guest house to the Abbey and was not dedicated as a church until *c*.1237. The sheer size of it all is awesome (*see picture over page*). Originally eight bays, now only seven: the W door has probably been reset. The font may well have been in this first church. The nave is magnificent with bold carving on the capitals. Both N and S aisles are much later and the windows are in the Perpendicular style of the 15th century. Many windows (*c*.1920) from the workshop of Morris & Co.; also some 16th century continental glass. The tower is a late 17th century addition, but there is evidence of the reuse of 13th century materials.

RAMSEY St. MARY *St. Mary* [C4]
A large Victorian church, built in 1858 at the expense of Miss Emma Fellowes. Corbels in the roof of kings and queens. Good font with scenes from the life of Christ, and large angels support the chancel arch.

REACH *Holy Trinity* [F6]

A chantry chapel dedicated to St. Etheldreda is recorded in Reach in 1378. Little is known of that building until 1768 when a drawing showed the chapel in ruins, parts of which can be seen beside the present church. Holy Trinity was built in 1861 to serve as church and school. This it did until 1909 when a separate school was built; at which time the priest-in-charge noted "Church clear of Day-school. Thank God!" The elegant 18th century font and the lectern came from the now disused church of St. Cyriac and St. Julitta at Swaffham Prior.

St Ives

ST. IVES *All Saints* [D]

A fine church. The graceful steeple has had an eventful existence and has been rebuilt on three occasions; the last time after a Royal Flying Corps plane flew into it in 1918. Walk round and admire the W door before entering by the N porch. The Early English piscina in the S aisle is similar to those in Jesus College, Histon and Hemingford Grey. The major part of the building was completed in the latter part of the 15th century and is a good example of the Perpendicular period. The elaborate screen, organ

Ramsey~St Thomas

74

case and loft are particularly early examples of the work of Sir Ninian Comper, from 1893. Other windows are by Comper and Kempe. In the nave statues of saints, again by Comper (c.1897); they stand on 15th century corbels. The pulpit is Elizabethan. Before you leave St. Ives, visit the tiny chapel on the narrow medieval bridge. It was dedicated to St. Laurence and consecrated in 1426, and is one of only three such "Bridge Chapels" in the country.

ST. NEOTS *St. Mary* [B6]
A walk along the wide path surrounding the church enables you to appreciate that the church and its spectacular tower are of one uniform style: the Perpendicular period of the late 15th and early 16th centuries. The flat nave roof was a late medieval fashion. The tower, one of the very best in the county, was begun in the 1480s, and took 50 years to complete. Inside are wonderful roofs, screens, ornate carvings of all manner of angels and beasts, an elegant niche by the north door and fascinating monuments, especially the one to the Rowleys. Most of the benches are 19th century though there are several medieval ones with misericords. Much Victorian glass, especially by Clayton & Bell.

SAWSTON *St. Mary the Virgin* [E8]
Three pleasantly ugly gargoyles face the street and there are excellent corbels inside. The tall round arches W of the nave remain from the sizable Norman building. The chancel may be 13th century and there are several lancet windows. On the S side two large Perpendicular windows were inserted later but half of one lancet remains. Several good brasses, especially that of Robert Lockton and his wife (1500). Also interesting graffiti on a round pillar of N aisle: one of a man wearing a little pointed cap thought to be 12th century; one about 15 inches high of a man holding a sword, thought by T. C. Lethbridge to be connected with the hill figures he discovered on the nearby Gogmagog Hills.

SAWTRY *All Saints* [B4]
Three churches were recorded in Sawtry in the 11th century. Little remains of the ruined St. Andrew's to the East of the A1

and nothing survives of the church at Sawtry Judith. All Saints, designed by Sir Arthur Blomfield, was built in the 1880s and much material was used from the earlier church. Medieval tiles were retained as well as some of the stained glass. The superb brass of Sir William le Moyne and his wife (1404) brings many visitors here.

St Neots

Shepreth

SHUDY CAMPS *St. Mary* [G8]

Little remains of the 13th century church except the S door of the chancel. Most of what you see now is the result of a major rebuilding programme in the 15th century and later. The chancel arch is curiously off-centre due to the nave being enlarged to the south. The rood screen (*c.*1920) is a World War I memorial. The Dayrells were Lords of the Manor from 1702 and there are monuments to various members of the family. Over the W door of the tower are figures of the Virgin and Child and St. George.

SIX MILE BOTTOM *St. George* [F7]

The foundation stone was laid in April 1933 and this neat little church, built in flint and brick, was consecrated in December of the same year. The land was given for the church by the Delamere family, twenty years earlier. The curious twisted wooden pillars were given by Lady Delamere and may be of French origin; the lovely little font echoes the design of the canopy and pillars under which it stands.

SNAILWELL *St. Peter* [G6]

A Cambridgeshire round tower is a rare thing; the only other one is at Bartlow, though they are more plentiful elsewhere in East Anglia. The nave stands almost as tall as the 12th century tower. Inside, a picture shows a very different interior before the Victorian restoration, but the screens with gilded ornament remain from the medieval building. Early English lancets. The more elaborate design of the arch above the tomb-chest, perhaps earlier used as an

Snailwell

SHEPRETH *All Saints* [D8]

A peaceful setting overlooking open countryside. A lovely interior: the small Norman chancel arch seems just the right scale. On either side of the arch are decorative altar recesses of the 13th century. The piscina is also 13th century but the chancel has been rebuilt on three occasions: in the 17th, 18th and 19th centuries. In 1743 the tower cracked, perhaps struck by lightning or as a result of damage from the hurricane two years previously. In 1774 the spire was dismantled and the tower lowered in 1853. The uniqueness of All Saints is perhaps not only in the bricks and mortar but in the atmosphere of it all.

Snailwell

Easter Sepulchre, and the niches in the chancel are Decorated. Notice also the ornate cross set into the S arcade. Lovely hammerbeam roof with large figures of bishops on one side and saints on the other.

SOHAM St. Andrew [F5]

A church has been standing on this site since 650, when Felix of Burgundy built a monastery here. The 13th century church was cruciform with a central tower, and the great pillars that supported it remain. There is lavish decoration on the W side of the W arch. The superb W tower you see now was "new" in 1502 and is a very fine example of the Perpendicular period, possibly by a Suffolk architect. Notice the flushwork around the base, in particular the intricate designs on the N side, the same side as the elaborate N porch. It seems that the masons were quite unable to hold themselves back when decorating the top stages of the tower. Admire the angels in the hammerbeam roof and the lovely ogee-decorated piscina and sedilia in the 14th century chancel. Some medieval glass remains in the Lady Chapel; notice the little panes of birds in the N window. The medieval pews are now at the W end of the nave. Look closely at the fine 16th century screen in the N transept; it is the original rood screen and stood under the chancel arch until the mid-19th century restoration.

Soham

Several of the little faces are similar to those in the rood screen across the fen at Chippenham, but there is a curled up crocodile here too. A memorial in the N aisle to the railwaymen who saved this small town from a burning ammunition train in 1944; two were awarded the George Cross.

SOMERSHAM St. John the Baptist [D5]

The Bishops of Ely had a palace in Somersham for centuries and they may well have paid for this fine Early English church, mostly built between 1250 and 1300. In the chancel three slender lancets, the piscina and triple sedilia remain from that early building. The glass is a memorial to those who died during World War I. The medieval nave roof has splendid carved bosses, one of King Richard II and another of his wife, Anne of Bohemia; they must have been spectacular when brightly painted. There are remains of medieval wall decoration above the N door. Note too the strongly carved corbels: one man sits cross-legged, another strokes his beard. 16th century brass in chancel floor.

Southoe

SOUTHOE *St. Leonard* [B6]

The more you look at the Norman S doorway the more amazing it becomes, resembling a sampler of the craftsman's skills; the 12th century mason demonstrating all the designs in his repertoire. He continued in less exuberant fashion on the interior of the doorway. The chancel arch is also Norman, but the lancet windows are later, Early English. Merton College has long been the Patron of St. Leonard's and the brickwork of the Elizabethan tower and clerestory gives the church a pleasantly formal air.

SPALDWICK *St. James* [B5]

Another good Huntingdon shire tower and broach spire, over 150 feet tall. The W door of the tower and the large diamond shaped windows above are characteristic of the later Decorated period (*c.*1340). Continue around to the N doorway which is Norman. The 13th century chancel windows are very fine; the S arcade has nailhead decoration on the capitals (*c.*1200). Snail shells are used here too as decoration, as the

Spaldwick

symbol of St. James, patron saint of pilgrims. A simple glazed pitcher, used as a flower vase, is a loving memorial to a victim of the Korean war.

STANGROUND *St. John the Baptist* [C3]

A pleasant uncomplicated church built towards the end of the 13th century and consecrated in 1310. The tower has ballflower frieze decoration of the 14th century and a broach spire. Much of interest inside: nice corbels on the piers - the one in the S aisle might be the work of an apprentice, and some of the menagerie on the capitals in the N aisle are rather tentative too. You can also find a splendid Green Man, and a corbel with a bald-headed man is said to represent the master mason. An unusual stone seat in the chancel, similar to those at Houghton and Farcet; also lovely double piscina and sedilia under one arch. In the tower some little brass hooks for the bell ropeswere given in 1930, one with the diesel symbol of the local engineering company. The stone cross in the churchyard is considered to be pre-Conquest.

STAPLEFORD *St. Andrew* [E7]

Lovely little flint church with chancel arch and some zigzag decoration remaining from the 12th century Norman building. The 13th century saw a rebuilding of the chancel and the Early English lancets were inserted. Modern craftsmen have left their mark here too. The glass in the E window of the S aisle is by Christopher Webb (1960); his symbol of St. Christopher can be seen. A statue of St. Andrew, by John Skelton (1963). In 1988 new tiles were laid around the font in a maze: start your journey from the centre of the W wall and when you reach the font, read the words (from T.S. Eliot's "Little Gidding") around the cover. The new organ, by William Johnson, was also dedicated in 1988. Fragments of a small Norman coffin and an earlier Saxon cross have survived from the earliest days of this lovely building.

STEEPLE GIDDING *St. Andrew* [B4]

A pleasant walk across the fields from Little Gidding brings you to this little church dating from the 12th century; the S doorway remains from that building. Walk around outside to the W and notice the unusually narrow tower and slender spire. Three curiosities here: the slit window in the W nave wall which may be a squint but seems too high; the strangely placed niche above the S belfry windows; and high on the buttress of the NE corner of the nave is a consecration cross, a rare survival of the original twelve. The Norman doorway, with round-headed outer arch and zigzag moulding, was moved during a 14th century rebuilding. Fine monument to Sir John Cotton (d.1752), recording his descent

Steeple Gidding

from David, King of Scotland. Interesting headstones in the churchyard. The building is now in the care of the Redundant Churches Fund.

STEEPLE MORDEN *St. Peter and St. Paul* [C8]

An unusual little flint church with much flushwork in the S buttresses. The original steeple collapsed in 1633 and the shingled one you see now was built in 1866. The rather casually blocked up windows of an earlier clerestory remain. Inside notice the quatrefoil design of the piers with drip moulding on the bases, late 13th and 14th centuries.

STETCHWORTH *St. Peter* [G7]

Down a quiet lane away from the village with a churchyard that is carpeted with snowdrops in early spring, an embattled tower, decorated with flushwork, bids you welcome. The strange round quatrefoil windows are from the 19th century restoration but the chancel still retains its Early English lancets. A lovely little niche in the S aisle has an angel which perhaps once supported a statue of St. Peter. A vast monument in N aisle to Henry Gorges, Superintendent of the Draining of the Great Level, dated 1674. A memorial nearby to Ashton Benyon who "drooped and died in manhood's early dawn." More cheerful reminders of earlier

Stilton

similar exaggerated attire. On the second pier, a man is shown in doublet, hose and pointed shoes as worn at the French court about the same time. Mrs. Pritchard, in her book *English Medieval Graffiti*, suggests that this may be connected with a visit of Queen Philippa, wife of Edward III, as it is known she stopped here on her journey to Norwich on several occasions.

STIBBINGTON *St. John the Baptist* [A3]
At first glance the church comes as a surprise with the three-gabled facade, a result of a major rebuilding in 1849, but the W door is Norman and inside much remains from the 12th century: the N arcade, chancel, chancel arch and octagonal font have stood here since then. Interesting memorial to Captain Wright, who fought at the Battle of Flamborough Head (1779). In the graveyard lies Canon Trollope, rector 1868-1907 and uncle of the novelist Anthony Trollope, a frequent visitor to the village.

STILTON *St. Mary* [B4]
Much restoration was carried out in the early part of the 19th century and the chancel was rebuilt. The nave and arcades are early 13th century; notice the different shapes of the piers: round on the S, and octagonal on the slightly earlier N arcade. The tower is later, the nailhead decoration on one of the capitals putting it at about 1300. Ornately carved lectern. Delightful brass to Yeoman Richard Curthoyse (1573) and his wife (1606). In the churchyard some very interesting tomb chests and headstones; French names must be of prisoners who were kept at Norman Cross during the Napoleonic wars.

STOW CUM QUY *St. Mary* [F6]
Little remains of the original small, aisleless church, but there is the outline of an earlier window in the S arcade near the chancel. The building was enlarged about 1340 and the window to the W of the N aisle has unique tracery of the Decorated period. The tower was added later that century. A short piece of dogtooth decoration from the earlier building is set into the SE pier, underneath two weary little heads. High in the nave you can just make out the remains of a medieval wall-painting of St.

worshippers can be found in their "scratchings" or graffiti on the piers of the N aisle. A lady is shown (3rd pier from the W) wearing a very elaborate head-dress (*c.*1330), and an owl-like creature above her, perhaps as a somewhat mocking cartoon, with

Christopher. Fine brass to John Anstey (1465), still watched by his twelve sons and four daughters, although two are hidden by the pulpit steps. A memorial in the S aisle to Jeremy Collier, eminent church historian and scourge of the Restoration playwrights. Another tells of the two priests from Stow who later became Archbishops.

Stow Longa

parts of the present building are the entrance doorway, which is Early Engl- ish, and the arcade. The tower is much later and can be dated, by the arms of a Bishop of Lincoln on the W wall, to 1496-1514. Two Mass dials are thought to be Saxon. There is much to admire, including the Early English font, in this interesting church tucked away at the end of the village.

Stow Longa

STOW LONGA St. Botolph [B5]
St. Botolph was an Abbot of a Suffolk monastery (some insist it was in Lincolnshire); he died in 680. The tympanum with the wild-looking mermaid was carved over the priest's door in the 12th century and must remain from an earlier church. The oldest

STRETHAM St. James [F5]
Saved from ruin in the last century when it was practically rebuilt; but much remains of the 14th century interior. Good 15th century Perpendicular rood screen, although the rood group is of the 20th century and was erected as a memorial to those who died in World War II. In the Lady Chapel read the poem by Innes Stitt who died aged 19 in the First World War. He was the rector's son, and his marble memorial is in the S wall of the chancel. Large brass to Joan Swan (d. 1497).

STUNTNEY Holy Cross [F5]
At first glance appears to be all Victorian but then you come to the S doorway: the rounded arch and zigzag decoration are all Norman. A vigorous rebuilding in the last century moved the Norman N doorway to its rather uneasy position in the S aisle; the original 12th century chancel arch was moved behind the organ at the same time. The font is also thought to date from the Norman church. Lovely stained glass window by John Hayward (1964), and nearby a 17th century alms box.

SUTTON Nr. Peterborough St. Michael [A3]
No tower, but the bellcote dates from the 13th century, as does the window below. Two rather startled faces greet you from high above the N doorway and inside more faces support the roof as corbels. But it is the rounded Norman chancel arch (c.1130) and

the marvellous carving on the capitals which dominate the interior. Also note the two splendid Green Men on the capitals. In the S aisle lies a passive lion which may once have been part of a Norman doorway.

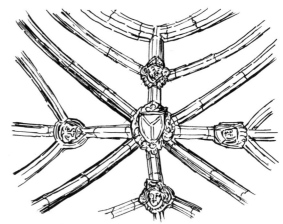

Sutton-in-the-Isle

Sutton-in-the-Isle

SUTTON-IN-THE-ISLE *St. Andrew* [D5]
The distinctive "pepperpot" tower is visible for miles. In fact the octagon shape from Ely Cathedral is repeated twice in the tower. Notice that the S, or 'show' side, is the most elaborate, with battlements, gargoyles and of course the wonderful two-storey porch. The whole church was probably rebuilt between 1350 and 1370. It is a marvellous example of the progression of the late Decorated period into the Perpendicular. The elaborate tracery in the windows, extravagant carving and the ogee arch are evidence of the early 14th century Decorated style. The beautiful E window in the chancel is a very early attempt at the Perpendicular style (the modern stained glass is also impressive). The medieval work was done in three stages: nave, chancel, tower. The architect also worked on important mid-Norfolk churches at Attleborough and Hingham. Admire the vaulted roof in the tower, the two-light clerestory windows, the blank arcading around the windows. Faces grin down at you everywhere, gargoyles, grotesques and corbel heads. In the S aisle a lovely corner piscina with a sadly mutilated Madonna. Interesting churchyard; a headstone to John Youndes, who fought at Waterloo and died in 1878 at the age of 82.

SWAFFHAM BULBECK *St. Mary* [F6]

Three stages of building can be distinguished fairly easily as you walk up to the church. The tower with narrow lancet windows is Early English, 13th century; you can see the outline of an earlier steep roofline on its eastern wall. The chancel has more elaborate windows with flowing tracery of the Decorated period and the ogee arch of the same period is used for the sedilia and tomb recess; the aisles and clerestory were added in the 15th century and the windows take on the more severe lines of the Perpendicular period. But that all sounds rather serious: inside you will find much light-hearted medieval craftsmanship. The carving of the bench ends is spectacular! No plain poppyheads here, but camels, a whale, a merman and what looks to be a close cousin of a turkey; and all this carving was done in the 15th century. A 15th century Italian chest in the S aisle was once used as a travelling altar. Some interesting 18th century headstones in the churchyard and a 13th century coffin lid being used as a stile.

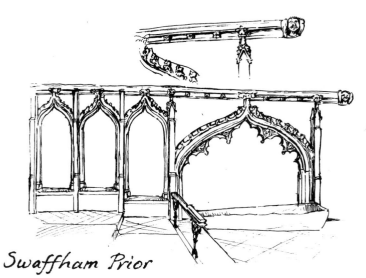

Swaffham Prior

Swaffham Prior

SWAFFHAM PRIOR *St. Mary. St. Cyriac & St. Julitta* [F6]

A rather astonishing sight - these two large churches standing side by side high above the village street. St. Mary's is the parish church in use today. The tower was built between 1150 and 1180; so the octagon stage predates that at Ely Cathedral. Inside you will find a typical feature of the 15th century in the lozenge shaped piers, elongated N to S. Some interesting portrait brasses, the oldest of John Tothyll (d. 1463). Windows in the S aisle came from St. Cyriac's. The unusual First World War memorial windows in the N aisle apparently caused "a considerable stir" when first seen. The church of St. Cyriac and his mother St. Julitta, built *c.*1250, was made redundant in 1972. Nothing remains of the 13th century building. The late 15th century tower is similar to that of St. Mary's - an octagon on a square base. The remainder results from rebuilding in 1809-11.

SWAVESEY *St. Andrew* [D6]

An impressive church in a large cedar-filled churchyard. There is some evidence of Saxon long-and-short work in the S chapel. Handsome early 14th century exterior. Inside there is a veritable forest of carved bench ends, almost all 19th century work. The smaller medieval benches are in the N aisle. Excellent misericords in the chancel include a falcon clutching a rabbit, two squirrels munching acorns and many others; all this watched over by medieval angels in the chancel roof. Contrast two very different styles of piscina and sedilia: Decorated, early 14th century with ogee arch, in the chancel; later, Perpendicular in the S chapel. Interesting Jesse Tree window in the Lady Chapel (1967), and a lovely monument by Edward Marshall (1631).

TADLOW *St. Giles* [C8]

Easy to miss this church, standing to the N of the main road, some way from the village. Mainly 13th century. The tower is later and money was left towards its building in 1472. All was restored in 1860 by William Butterfield. Inside the entrance doorway there is the almost obliterated indent of Margaret Broggrife (1493); a drawing in the tower shows her praying above her six children. William Dowsing came here in 1643 and recorded that he demolished two windows and a cross. A 17th century Archdeacon's Visitation recorded that during the sermon on Christmas Day a dog stole the consecrated bread from the Altar Table and consequently the priest did not feel he could offer Communion that day.

TEVERSHAM *All Saints* [E7]

Much remains of the Early English building. The tower is later in a typically East Anglian Perpendicular style. The capitals of the arcade have been dated *c.*1230. There is more bold design on the slender piers to the E. The clerestory, of the same period, once let the outside light shine through its strange oval eyes. The work of Victorian craftsmen must be admired in the chancel; their angels are linked with banners below the handsome roof. Lovely rood screen and Jacobean pulpit bought from St. Andrew's, Cherry Hinton in 1891. A tomb chest (1598) stands in the S aisle.

THORNEY *St. Mary and St. Botolph* [C2]

The first Minster was founded here in 662; it prospered, was sacked by the Danes and rebuilt in 972 as a Benedictine monastery sheltering the relics of three local saints. At the Dissolution by Henry VIII in 1530s this immense building was almost completely destroyed and its masonry and furnishings distributed throughout the county and beyond. What remains is the people's nave and the wonderful W front; the enormous 15th century window was replaced by a smaller one in 1638. The 15th century octagon turrets are linked by a series of statue-filled niches; the stairways remain from the Norman building. Walk around the outside to get an idea of the size of the arcades before the destruction took place. The interior is now tall and narrow, focusing on the rich

Thorney

colours of the E window which was installed in 1840, a copy of one in Canterbury Cathedral. The transepts were also added at this time.

THORNHAUGH *St. Andrew* [A2]

Stands high above the road in a lovely churchyard filled with early headstones carved with skulls, cherubs and urns; all now softened with lichen and moss. The low tower was built in 1889 and replaced an earlier tower which fell in the 15th century. Bright medieval decoration can still be seen on the arcades. The Early English chancel retains its lancet windows and dogtooth ornament around the piscina. In the Chantry Chapel is the splendid Russell Monument: the tomb of Sir William Russell, created the first Baron Russell of Thornhaugh in 1603. He died in 1613 in Hertfordshire and was buried here. His effigy is surrounded by his three brothers and three sisters kneeling in prayer. In 1694 this Sir William's grandson was created 1st Duke of Bedford.

THRIPLOW *St. George or All Saints* [E8]

Attractive cruciform church, easily seen long before you reach the village. William Cole visited here in 1742 and recorded several medieval stained glass windows, some "very well done", and painted panels on the screen. Later restorations have removed much of it, and only fragments of the once lovely screen, (*c.*1350) remain. It was a particularly good example of its kind and in 1518 the church of Great St. Mary in Cambridge ordered their new screen to be similar to that at Thriplow. In the chancel is a double piscina, with central flutings or grooves. The delicately painted roofs are Victorian, perhaps from the time of Gilbert Scott's restoration in 1877. Stand beneath the crossing and see the medieval faces at each corner.

Tilbrook

TILBROOK *All Saints* [A6]

A lovely place with much of interest. The 13th century building may have had a central tower but this

Tilbrook

collapsed, to be replaced by the fine Decorated W tower with a broach spire and splendid gargoyles too. Above the entrance to the porch there is a figure said to be St. Anthony and a pig. The round piers in the N arcade are Norman, late 12th century. Wonderful rood screen with some original paintwork, hinting at the brilliance and colour once enjoyed in the earlier churches. Sections of the screen are now in the Victoria and Albert Museum. A very deep opening in the N wall of the chancel may have been the chrismatory to hold the requisites for baptism.

TOFT *St. Andrew* [D7]

Lovely churchyard, filled with snowdrops in February. The neat, brown cobble church has been subject to so much restoration and rebuilding that little remains of the medieval building but there is a lovely atmosphere here. In 1647 William Dowsing and his men visited during their tour of destruction and much damage was done. In the chancel mutilated figures remain from what must have been a beautiful 15th century alabaster altar.

TOSELAND *St. Michael* [C6]

The rounded arches of the S doorway, a window and the chancel arch remain from the Norman church. The list of rectors goes back to 1232 when the patron was the Bishop of Lincoln. Like so many others, the building fell into great disrepair in the last century. In 1873 Arthur Blomfield was responsible for the sympathetic restoration. A Sarsen stone, a pre-Christian megalith, stands near the entrance and once marked the meeting place of the Toseland Hundred.

TRUMPINGTON *St. Mary and St.Michael* [E7]

A parish church built almost on cathedral scale in the early part of the 14th century. A chapel once stood against the N wall of the chancel and its piscina remains on the outside wall. The chancel was built about 1280 and the narrow late Early English windows remain. The intricate E window is in the Decorated style of the early 14th century and fragments of medieval glass have

Trumpington

been assembled in a "grande salade." All is light and space. The font has quaint early 14th century faces on the bases, but stem and bowl are later and much recut. More medieval faces now support a 17th century tablet in the S transept, the woman's headdress indicating a date of *c.*1370. The pulpit, originally a "three-decker", was bought from Emmanuel College in 1677.

However, it is surely the large monument and important brass of Sir Robert de Trumpington (d.1289) that bring most visitors here; it is the second largest brass in England. Sir Roger lies under an elaborate ogee canopy, also contemporary with the rest of the building. The trumpet on his shield is repeated in medieval glass in the N aisle. Much restoration was carried out by William Butterfield between 1858 and 1867, including resurfacing the exterior with Bath stone.

Tydd St Giles

Trumpington

TYDD St. GILES *St. Giles* [E1]

An unusual and interesting church. The Early English tower stands alone, not unusual in the fenland where the greater weight of the tower makes them settle too deep and they can begin to lean crazily, as at Surfleet in Lincolnshire. Enter through the W door and notice above it the "Walsingham Window", said to have been designed by Alan of Walsingham, sacrist at Ely Cathedral and responsible for building the Octagon there after the collapse of the central tower in 1322. The interior of St. Giles is light, with stout 12th century arcades and different decoration for almost each capital. There really is no chancel. Sir Gilbert Scott, while his brother was rector here, took down the poorly built 18th century chancel which replaced the medieval chancel which had been destroyed during a gale in 1741. The font is lovely: the carving includes a grotesque, with mouth agape, said to represent Gluttony; an angel; a small Green Man with large foliage; the three crowns of Ely; St. George's shield and the symbols of the Passion.

UFFORD *St. Andrew* [A2]

Large double E windows dominate the approach, the result of the 19th century restoration. A walk around the outside reveals the remains of a 13th century piscina and little shelf from before the demolition of the N chapel; there is a low side window and niche here too. The handsome 15th century tower is of three stages, divided by a string-course and little battlements. The battlements are repeated again on the capitals of the tower arch inside. The high grand chancel arch of *c*.1300, is flanked by doorways which once opened onto the rood loft and up into the roof. The elegant arcades are a little later with

Ufford

small corbels as heads; there is a crowned lady with veil or a gossip's scold, next to a man who appears to be doing all the talking. Lovely details on the well-carved bench ends, some of them medieval. Notice the monument to the remarkable Lady Carre (d.1621), who was 25 years Gentlewoman to the Privy Chamber of Elizabeth I, and then served King James I's Queen Anne for a further 14 years.

UPTON Nr. Alconbury *St. Margaret* [B5]

An attractive, compact church. Weather-beaten gargoyles peer down from the strangely short broach spire. The S doorway and elaborate font are both Norman. The chancel is Early English with familiar Y-tracery windows. A major restoration was carried out in 1870 by Gilbert Scott and the N aisle added at this time. Outside, the little faces on the hood-moulds are 19th century too. Several 18th century monuments in the tower. A medical student, aged 25, died in 1802 in the "flower of his youth", and his epitaph ends "Go thy way Traveller, And convinced of the instability of Human Life, Meditate upon Eternity." Remains of the churchyard cross stand near the S porch.

UPTON Nr. Peterborough *St. John the Baptist* [B2]

An earlier dedication was to St. Helen, mother of the Emperor Constantine. This is a tranquil place, set in fields north of the A47. Notice particularly the straight-headed windows of the early 17th century rebuilding. The unspoilt interior is dominated by the Norman chancel arch (*c*.1120) and then by the massive altar tomb of Sir William Dove (d.1627). He lies beside his two wives; Dame Frances' hand is closed, but Dame Dorothy's lies open as a symbol of her known generosity and kindness to the poor. There is a very fine Jacobean pulpit and Communion Rails. In a field to the south stands a large 17th century sundial.

UPWOOD *St. Peter* [C4]

Much rebuilding has been necessary over the past hundred years. However, many features of the 12th century Norman church remain: round headed windows; round piers; a rounded chancel arch. The S arcade is later. Some medieval glass fragments also survive. Above the S door read the will of the generous Mrs. West. A "plague pit" is said to lie west of the churchyard. William Cromwell, cousin of Oliver, is said to have brought the plague to the area when he had a piece of cloth sent to him from London in 1666.

WANSFORD *St. Mary* [A3]
This attractive stone village straddled the Great North Road for centuries and the stone bridge over the Nene has seven arches surviving dated 1577, others from 17th and 18th centuries. The handsome church stands surrounded by lovely weathered headstones; one dated 1672 stands at a corner near the chancel E wall. The tower is 13th century but a triangular topped Saxon window survives in the W wall. The S doorway is

Wansford

c.1200 and the font is even earlier, about 1120. It is quite spectacular, with figures carved under the round Norman arches. It was found nearby at Sibberton Lodge being used as a cattle trough, on the site of a village abandoned after the plague. Rebuilding of the nave and porch was carried out in 1663 and the chancel was rebuilt in 1902.

WARBOYS *St. Mary Magdalene* [D4]
The handsome tower and broach spire, one of the very finest examples in the area, were completed by the end of the 13th century; the details of the bell openings and lucarnes are especially fine. Marvellous Norman chancel arch with bold zigzag decoration. The arcades are typical 13th century, with alternate round and octagonal piers in the N, S all rounded. The chancel was rebuilt in 1832, rather surprisingly in yellow brick. The

priest's door has what may be a rare 12th century door knocker of a lion's head and two dragons entwined in battle. Two good 18th century monuments by Bacon; one for Elizabeth Strode (1790), whose "anxious Endeavours to relieve Distress were not less judicious than liberal."

WARESLEY *St. James* [C7]
In 1724 the church was destroyed by "a tempest" and rebuilt four years later. It was again in poor repair in the last century and was replaced by the building you see now, designed by William Butterfield in 1856. The chancel is a fine example of his work. Contemporary stained glass; strong colours of the N aisle window in the Burne-Jones style. The church's battle with the elements continued when in January 1988 the entire spire was torn off during a violent storm. Less than six months later, as a result of heroic fundraising and labour, a Thanksgiving service was held to celebrate the rebuilding of Butterfield's elegant oak shingle spire. The Duncombe Mausoleum connects with the church to the south.

WATERBEACH St. John [E6]
Completed in the 13th century, and pillars in the N arcade have the stiff, upright leaves of c.1200. The S aisle and clerestory were 15th century additions. Early in the 19th century the spire collapsed for a second time and prolonged restoration took place. The chancel was completely rebuilt and the colour and decoration is typical of this Victorian period. The pulpit (1883) has elaborate mosaic panels. The Communion Table is by Rattee & Kett (1879), using a slab of Purbeck marble thought to be 11th century and found beneath a Tudor floor. The Revd. William Cole was Curate-in-Charge here from 1767 to 1770. He travelled tirelessly throughout the county and beyond, documenting and drawing the parish churches. Walk about 100 yards to the east to the Garden of Remembrance, there you will find the original 14th century font.

WATER NEWTON *St. Remigius* [B3]
The most picturesque way to approach this church would surely be by boat along the Nene. Ermine Street, the Roman road from

Water Newton

London to Lincoln, crossed the river not far from here. On the W face of the tower a niche holds a small kneeling figure, and the inscription below asks you to pray for the soul of Thomas Purdew. Early English tower and much of the interior as well. The list of rectors goes back to 1245. Restoration was carried out in the 17th century and most of the windows are from this period. Notice the carvings on the choir stalls, some with very aquiline profiles. There is a the stone effigy (c.1300) in the S aisle. The unusual dedication must refer to St. Remigius, the 6th century Bishop of Rheims who baptized Clovis, King of the Franks and all his followers. In 1975 a hoard of late Roman Christian silver, probably 4th century, was found at Water Newton. So a Christian community existed here before that. Simon Cotton suggests that a sub-Roman Christian community may have persisted here; or perhaps Remigius was an import of the Saxon period, or the dedication of an earlier church may have been changed to Remigius by 11th or 12th century Normans. To the S of the chancel lies the tomb of Admiral Edward Edwards (d. 1813); as Captain Edwards, he went out to capture the mutineers of the Bounty. He was shipwrecked and made a passage of 1000 miles to safety in an open boat.

WENTWORTH *St. Peter* [D5]
Two Norman doorways, the S being more elaborate than the N. In the chancel is an important early Norman sculpture of St. Peter, the figure very fresh looking. The font is 13th century with stiff-leafed decoration below the bowl. The Revd. Oswald Henry Moseley made the simple cross above the screen in 1890 and was

buried in the churchyard in 1899. In the tower a small tablet (1809) remembers Peppercorn Sanxter but does not tell us why.

WERRINGTON *St. John the Baptist* [B2]
A largely Norman building with a little twin bell-cote between nave and chancel roofs, zigzag decoration on the S doorway and nailhead ornament on some of the capitals. The chancel is Decorated and has a lovely E window; but it was all much restored in 1901-2. The porch, with stone seats, is also Decorated. A tablet on W end of the nave marks a restoration of 1680 and then again in 1884.

WESTLEY WATERLESS *St. Mary the Less* [G7]
This was the third church with a round tower in Cambridgeshire until it fell in 1855 (two others remain at Bartlow and Snailwell).

Wentworth

The church is justly famous for the exquisite brasses of Sir John Creke and his wife (1325) with "engraving of the highest distinction" (Alec Clifton-Taylor). Most of the building is in the Early English style of the 13th century. Unusual graffiti in the upper S window of the S aisle record, in early Arabic, the produce from various vines growing around the church. The church leaflet tells more. The cheerful painted organ was given "in token of loving friendship between the American and English people in 1968."

89

Weston Colville

WESTON COLVILLE *St. Mary* [G7]

A neat looking church with grey brick framing the flint work, and a tidy outline to tower and chancel; the result of rebuilding about 1825. The porch is late medieval and some evidence of the 14th century interior remains, notably the chancel arch. Two good brasses: Abraham Gates with his wife (1636); also Robert Leverer (1427), who stands in a field of cheerful flowers, with his wife beside him, and their son, a priest. All watched over by angels high in the E windows, each with a musical instrument.

WEST WICKHAM *St. Mary* [G8]

Set in a picturesque churchyard almost on the Suffolk border. The interior is painted a cheerful pink throughout, which particularly enhances the early 14th century chancel and the very tall chancel arch. Above the arch hangs the Royal Coat of Arms of Queen Anne dated 1708. Notice the medieval timber roof, and the delicate carving on one massive beam. Several medieval benches survive and a sturdy parish chest.

WEST WRATTING *St. Andrew* [G7]

The 14th century building was 'modernized' in 1746 and then again in 1896. The elegant iron screen is a more recent addition of 1922; beside it notice the doorway to the original rood loft which must have been quite massive and well forward of the chancel arch. Lovely high timber roof with elegant bosses. The 18th century font, used as a flower holder, now stands upside down near the north wall of the chancel. Beside it read the complicated memorial to Annie Walker (d. 1610) "both she and her mother saw her daughter's daughter's daughter ..." Stained glass (1910) by Morris & Co.

Whaddon

WHADDON *St. Mary* [D8]

Handsome flint and pebble church with battlements all around. The chancel dates to about 1300; notice the dogtooth moulding on the E side of the arch. Large two-tiered aisle windows lighten the nave, and the tall arcades are *c*.1375. The E window is later and restored. Note the altar tomb for John d'Eschallers (1469). The family were Lords of the Manor for 400 years and their arms are also on the font. Read of the history of the Hatchment of the 3rd Earl Hardwicke. The organ with its mighty angel with gilded trumpet was installed in 1832.

Whittlesey-St Mary

WHITTLESEY *St. Andrew* [C3]

Not as grand as St. Mary's on the other side of town, but this is a fine church surrounded on three sides by a park-like churchyard. Tower and porch are both early 16th century; notice the Tudor rose on the W door. There are chapels to N and S of the chancel, all with original roofs. Look at the piers in the nave, lozenge-shaped N to S, typical of the Perpendicular building of the 15th century. Lovely tracery in the chancel E window. A tall wooden angel holds the lectern and there is good 20th century carving on the pulpit. Interesting memorial (1703) to the rector of both Whittlesey churches.

WHITTLESEY *St. Mary* [C3]

One of the very best Perpendicular spires in the country dates from *c.*1450, probably based on Northamptonshire designs. Stand back in the great churchyard and admire the large window an elaborate doorway. No expense was spared with the building of the tower and the crocketed spire, the four flying buttresses and elegant corner pinnacles. Inside, the N arcade and chancel arch are 13th century, the Early English period. The S aisle and chapel are in the more flamboyant Decorated style. The raised part of the chapel once had an altar but only the piscina remains; the crypt below was the charnel-house. In the chancel read the memorial to Elizabeth Kentish. Underneath is an empty monument to the Hake family (1590), supporters of the Royalist cause; the kneeling figures were probably destroyed during the Common-wealth.

WHITTLESFORD *St. Mary and St. Andrew* [E8]

A lovely little church with 12th century nave and central tower. In the S aisle there is a pictorial history of the building. Alabaster fragments from a medieval altar were found only 100 years ago. Many benches with medieval carving. The wall-paintings

Whittlesford

'Sheela-na-gig' lintol

Porch rafters.

Whittlesford

AES 89

were discovered in 1905 and are thought to be part of a Doom, the shield of the Scaler family and a pattern of pomegranates. There is also fine 13th century ornament on the N side of the chancel. The four pillared font also dates from the Early English period. Graffiti of an archer on the pillar next to the pulpit. Outside, notice the strange 12th century carving of a sheila-na-gig built decorously high on the tower below the clock. Also see the tomb of the Hollicks family, who, as Nonconformists, were buried just outside the churchyard; but they made sure that the handsome stone urn would draw attention to their high standing in the community.

WICKEN *St. Laurence* [F5]

A quiet unpretentious village church built surprisingly close to the fen, perhaps to take advantage of the convenience of transportation of the building materials. The simple interior is largely 14th century and the nave is quite broad; six sturdy heads support the medieval roof. Three generations of Oliver Cromwell's family are buried here. Two small but elegant brasses to Margaret Peyton (d. 1414) and John Peyton (d. 1520).

WILBURTON *St. Peter* [D5]

There are two porches and the N porch has two storeys. A dignified interior with fine large 15th century windows outlined by blind arcading in nave and chancel. A cockerel hangs high in the nave roof and this emblem is continued elsewhere in the roof and rood screen, showing the patronage here of Bishop Alcock of Ely. Thomas Alcock, related to the Bishop, was rector here in 1496 and was probably responsible for part of the rebuilding of the nave roof. Very fine brasses now hang on the walls. Faded 15th century wall-paintings show two Bishops - one may be St. Blaise, who with St. Leger is a patron saint of woolcombers; St. Christopher can only be seen very faintly. The N transept has various monuments to the Pell family. Note the 20th century "Gothic" monument.

Wilburton

WILLINGHAM St. Mary and All Saints [D5]

You are greeted by cheerful gargoyles outside and marvellous wall-paintings throughout the interior; also a quite spectacular nave roof, almost bursting with angels. The stone porch is early 14th century, as is much of this handsome church. The building and land surrounding were given to Ely before the Conquest and this may account for the extravagance of some of the later building. The church was used for large ordination services in the 14th century. In the chancel are triple sedilia and a piscina, the typically Decorated ogee arch over the

Willingham

Willingham

Easter Sepulchre and again over a tomb recess in the N parclose. The screens, still colourful, stretch across nave and aisles. The very unusual stone vaulted sacristy to the NE of the chancel may have been a treasury as well as a chapel. It has very small windows which were originally protected by iron bars and the stone ribs are built as imitation wooden trusses. The church was in a ruinous state in the last century. In 1890 the Revd. John Watkins undertook

a major restoration and the wall-paintings were discovered at this time. Pamela Tudor-Craig suggests that the figure of St. Etheldreda (c.1300) may be the earliest surviving wall-painting representation of the saint. The splendid St. Christopher was painted at least a century later. Notice particularly the Visitation scene (perhaps 15th century), high in the SE corner or the nave. Both Mary and Elizabeth are highly pregnant and are wearing maternity dresses with expandable cross laced fronts.

WIMBLINGTON St. Peter [E3]

This was the first church in the village and was designed in 1874 by Thomas Henry Wyatt, replacing an earlier chapel. A sturdy cruciform building with low tower and spire. Elegant ironwork for the screen and communion rail and a fine W window as a memorial for villagers who died in World War I. Several interesting 19th and 20th century headstones in the churchyard.

WIMPOLE St. Andrew [D8]

The church was the centre of the medieval village of which nothing survives; the whole village was moved out of sight during the 18th century landscaping of the park. The interior is perhaps not what you expect to find in a country church; all that remains of the medieval building is the 14th century N chapel, now a treasure-house of monuments and memorials. Sir Thomas Chicheley, an ardent Royalist (d.1616), his wife and their six children surround the large alabaster table-tomb. There are several monuments to the Earls of Hardwicke, owners of the Hall in the 18th and 19th

Wimpole

centuries; many devoted their lives to public office. One spectacular window is filled with 14th century heraldic glass. The 19th century W window of the N chapel shows what appears to be Prince Albert. Nave and chancel were rebuilt in 1749 by Flitcroft, the architect who had also largely rebuilt the Hall. However, a late Victorian restoration took place, and Pevsner says "little survives inside of the good manners of the 18th century, and the West gallery of 1887 ... leaves one bewildered."

WINWICK *All Saints* [B4]

Another handsome Huntingdonshire tower. It has an unusual little S door with heavy moulding which then continues around the tower. The main S doorway has been here since the 12th century and the chancel, with two lancet windows, is a century later. A lovely window of the Decorated period at the E end of the N transept, but the windows beside it to the N are later. Several interesting contemporary wall-paintings: Christ the Sower and others by Hamish Moyle; in the S transept the Creation by Elizabeth Tudor-Craig is flooded with light from the tall Perpendicular window.

WISBECH *St. Augustine* [E2]

A fine Victorian church designed by W. Basset-Smith in 1867 and consecrated in 1869. Basset-Smith had earlier been involved with the restoration of St. Peter and St. Paul in Wisbech. Light and welcoming interior with whitewashed walls and stripped pine pews. In 1953 a simple reredos, by David Roberts of Cambridge, as a memorial to those who died in World War II, was erected in front of the more ornate original. Traces of 19th century painted panels of St. Augustine and St. Monica can just be seen on either side of the large E window.

WISBECH *St. Peter and St. Paul* [E2]

A curious building indeed. The rather grand tower with battlements and pinnacles is set apart from the main building. It dates from about 1525 when the Norman tower collapsed. The interior becomes more complicated still, with two naves and two aisles. The Norman arcade remains from the 12th century church.

There have been many additions and rebuildings over the centuries resulting in windows and arches being off-centre, and what is known as the "crank" between the chancel arch and the Norman arcade. A very fine brass (1401) lies in the chancel floor; there are also several elaborate 17th century monuments here which may draw your attention to the fact that the chancel walls slope to the outside. For all that, it is a fine place with much of interest.

WISBECH ST. MARY *St. Mary* [E2]

Late 14th century, extended later when the characteristic 15th century clerestory was added. Beside the font, a very rare 20th century brass commemorates Canon Mowbray Smith, shown as a young man in Mass vestments. He was vicar here from 1914 until 1951. The church is filled with statues, carvings and medieval glass all collected by the indefatigable Mowbray Smith. He found the lectern in Suffolk, said to have been part of the figurehead of a 16th century Spanish ship, but probably of later, Low Countries' origin. He saved the Sanctus bell, which was being used as a gas alarm, from a ruined church in World War I. The helmet which saved his own life has a place of honour here too. Don't miss the corbels in the S aisle. Allow yourself time to enjoy this very lovely church and to admire what has been described as all its "Bon Dieuserie."

WISTOW *St. John the Baptist* [C4]

Don't let the gargoyles deter you from enjoying this interesting church. Its mid-16th century tower may have been completed after the Reformation. The stone-masons were given free rein here: there are gargoyles all round the exterior and a lion lies curled around the SW corner. Inside too there are faces or animals on corbels on the arcades, in the aisles; no suitable place has been left empty. Detailed craftsmanship everywhere: early 14th century ironwork on the S door; dark carved figures of saints almost hidden in the nave roof. In the chancel roof the angels are more easily visible, supported on stone corbels; here also the ogee arch, used to such great effect by masons during the Decorated period, over the sedilia and low side window. The medieval rood screen

largely 13th century, as can be seen by the Y-tracery in the lancet windows in the W tower and chancel. Much brickwork patching has been used over the years. Rebuilding of the tower was completed in 1691 and the date is carved in the W wall. Inside, notice the outline of an earlier and much larger arch. Good corbels in the nave roof, especially the bearded man with

skinny legs to the N of the chancel arch. Rare 15th century stone pulpit and a finely carved font of about 1300. The glass in the E window is by Geoffrey Webb (1946); his symbol is in the lower right corner.

Wistow

now stands in the S aisle. Fragments of carving by Norman masons have been set in the S wall. The highlight is surely the 15th century window in the S aisle; it was once part of the E window, but has somehow survived several periods of destruction and was lovingly restored in the last century. It shows the Annunciation; also the Resurrection scene where, unusually, Christ is shown stepping onto the near prostrate centurion as he leaves the tomb. This scene was taken from a text used in several medieval Mystery plays.

WITCHAM *St. Martin* [E4]
The unusual dedication to this 4th century apostle of Touraine usually indicates a pre-Conquest church. The present building is

Witcham

WITCHFORD *St. Andrew* [F5]
An alarming lean to the short tower, but it has been here since the 13th century. Three stone faces, perhaps from an earlier building, are let into the outside walls. The Witchford Lion is a fine piece of Norman sculpture and looks down from above the lancet window to the W of the porch. A primitive bearded face can be found on the chancel S wall, and a happier cherub Witchford

below the E window. The consecration date of the church is known to be 1376. In the chancel the delicate colours can still be seen around the piscina. A modern window shows St. Joseph teaching carpentry to the Boy Jesus, a fitting memorial to a past carpenter-churchwarden. High in a N window a foundering ship is an equally suitable memorial to John Townsend, lost at sea in 1872.

Wittering

WITTERING *All Saints* [A2]
The short rather upright building, with 13th century tower, does not prepare you for the splendour of the interior. The nave and chancel are still much as they were when built in the 11th century. The awesome proportions of the massive but simple chancel arch dominate this small pre-Conquest parish church; the arch may have been built after the Conquest but in the Saxon tradition. The 12th century Norman arcades seem almost over-decorated in comparison. On the outside of the chancel E wall there is a good example of the long-and-short work used by the Saxon masons. The Royal Air Force Commemorative Chapel was dedicated in 1968. The window above, by H. W. Harvey of York, shows St. Michael, the patron saint of the RAF. The candlesticks and crucifix were made in the station workshops, using metal from propeller blades. The chancel E window is by Kempe, complete with his wheatsheaf mark.

WOODHURST *St. John the Baptist* [D5]
A compact little church standing under silver birch trees. The N doorway remains from the Norman building, though it is blocked now and the octagonal font must be almost as old. The S arcade is 13th century. The sallow brick chancel was added in the 19th century but the more attractively coloured brick floor is a recent addition. On a wall at the W end of the churchyard, a 13th century coffin lid is used as coping. A lovely village with thatched houses and duck pond; the daffodils in the spring are dazzling.

WOOD DITTON *St. Mary* [G7]
Large flint church, mainly 16th century. The massive tower could certainly support a much larger belfry and steeple than the octagon it carries. The older nave roofline can be seen on the W face. The porch roof holds interesting figures and bosses and inside are some medieval alabaster fragments Medieval carving on some of the benches to the W of the nave, including a priest at prayer and a lamb. Fragments of wall-painting and faded colours of flowers and leaves still decorate the

Wood Ditton

Wood Ditton

WOODSTON *St. Augustine of Canterbury* [B3]

The dedication to St. Augustine may well relate to a very early Christian settlement. Much of what you see dates to the Victorian restoration, but in the W tower are fragments of Anglo-Saxon masonry and a small window of the same period. Two Saxon cemeteries were found nearby as well as evidence of Roman occupation. Several fine 17th and 18th century monuments hang in the aisles.

Woodston

Wood Walton

rood screen. Brasses in the S aisle to Henry English (1393) and his wife; he has a lion tucked under his spurs and her feet rest on a little dog with bells on its collar. A churchwarden of 1632 was remembered by his American descendants who placed a window in the chancel in his name in 1905. In the churchyard there is an epitaph for William Simmons, who "loved a sup in the dripping pan... but could not eat"; he died in 1753 and his dripping pan is embedded in the headstone.

WOOD WALTON *St. Andrew* [C4]

Looking from a distance like a child's drawing of a church, it stands on a hill some way from the village. Peter Bigmore suggests that it may have been sited centrally to serve several hamlets and possibly the situation was determined by the site being a much earlier heathen temple. Nowadays it is quite a landmark for travellers on the many trains that pass close by on the London-Scotland line. It is largely a 14th century building though the S arcade is Early English. In the 16th century the clerestory was added. A major rebuilding took place in 1859/60 when the aisles and tower were sympathetically rebuilt using much of the original materials. The church was declared redundant and since 1979 has been in the care of the Friends of Friendless Churches who have retiled the roof and installed vandal-proof glass. The medieval glass has been moved to the museum at Ely.

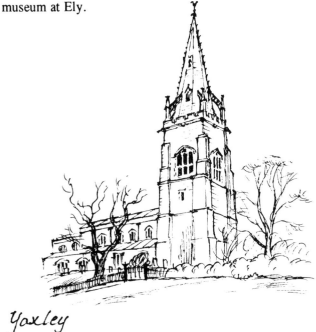

Yaxley

YAXLEY *St. Peter* [B3]
Wonderful late Perpendicular tower with airy flying buttresses supporting the recessed spire. Walk round the church and notice the different styles of tracery in the windows: plain Y-tracery of the 13th century; the E windows of S aisle and chancel, though restored, are full-blown Decorated (*c.*1330). The Perpendicular windows of clerestory and tower are more straightforward. The churchyard has risen so much over the centuries that you now walk down into the church itself; there is much of interest. Glass

in the chancel window by Sir Ninian Comper (1947, his strawberry symbol in one corner); you can read a detailed description of the window in the W end of the nave; the reredos and High Altar also by Comper. Fine medieval rood screen; remains of wall-paintings; details of a curious Heart Burial of 1293 in N transept and nearby a memorial to a "humane" Prison Commander paid for by French prisoners from the prison camp at Norman Cross during the Napoleonic Wars. The memorial on the site of the camp is on the west of the A1 just north of the Norman Cross roundabout.

YELLING *Holy Cross*
The dedication may remain from a pre-Conquest church, as the Saxons particularly venerated the Holy Cross. There was certainly a church here in 1086, a simple building of nave and chancel only. Stand in the nave and see the distinctive arcades in the N aisle (*c.*1180) with rounded piers and scalloped capitals. Compare with the S arcade of *c.*1300 when the usually severe Early English windows were given trefoil decoration. The 14th century saw a major building programme, including the tower, clerestory and enlargement of the chancel. Henry Venn, father of the founder of the Church Missionary Society, was rector here 1770-97. Early in the 19th century the spire was removed when it appeared to be in a state of imminent collapse on to the rectory.

Yaxley

GLOSSARY

AISLE see CHURCH PLAN

APSE A semi-circular or polygonal end.

ARCADE Range of arches supported on PIERS or columns. A blind-arcade, same attached to a wall.

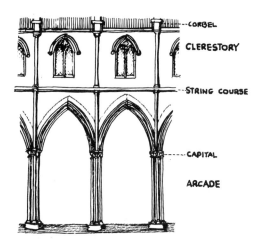

AUMBRY A recessed cupboard for the sacred vessels for Mass or Communion, usually on N wall of CHANCEL. Also used in some churches for the purpose of housing the reserved Sacrament.

BALLFLOWER Globular flower of three petals enclosing a small ball. Decoration used in the first quarter of the 14th century (DECORATED period).

BATTLEMENT a parapet with gaps at regular intervals (*see* drawing for QUOINS).

BOSS An ornamental projection, generally carved with foliage or figures, used to conceal the crossing of the ribs in a vaulted roof.

BROACH SPIRE *see* SPIRE.

CAPITAL Top or head of a column. (*see* drawing for ARCADE)

CHANCEL *see* CHURCH PLAN.

CHAPEL OF EASE A small building for worship other than the parish church.

CHANTRY CHAPEL Chapel attached to or inside a church, endowed for saying of Masses for the soul of the founder or another individual.

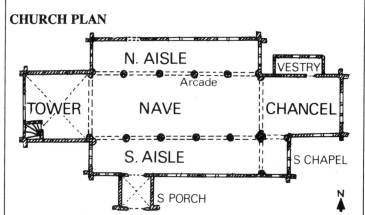

CHURCH PLAN

AISLE The side part of a church

CHANCEL The eastern compartment of the church beyond the nave, and housing the altar or communion table.

NAVE The main body of a church.

VESTRY A room in which robing takes place.

CHARNEL HOUSE A room, often below ground level, where the bones of the dead are deposited.

CHEVRON A zigzag ornamentation typical of the NORMAN period (*see* drawing for TYMPANUM).

CHRISMATORY Vessel for holding consecrated oil used in baptism, or cupboard for holding the vessel.

CLERESTORY The upper part of the NAVE and CHANCEL walls, containing a series of windows (*see* drawing for ARCADE).

CLUNCH a soft, chalky stone quarried in the SE of the county.

CORBEL Block of stone projecting just below the roof eaves externally or internally. Often adorned with carving (*see* drawing for ARCADE).

CROCKETS Decorative projections placed on sloping sides of SPIRES, pinnacles, gables (*see* drawing for SPIRE).

DECORATED ('DEC') Stylistic division of English GOTHIC architecture from *c.*1290 to *c.*1350 (*see* drawing for OGEE and TRACERY).

DOG-TOOTH Typical EARLY ENGLISH ornament, consisting of a series of raised four-cornered stars.

DRIP MOULDING *See* HOOD-MOULD.

EARLY ENGLISH Stylistic division of English GOTHIC architecture roughly covering the 13th century.

EASTER SEPULCHRE Recess to hold the consecrated Host prior to the Easter celebration. Usually in N CHANCEL wall.

ENTASIS The swelling of a column or SPIRE to prevent optical distortion.

FLUSHWORK Decorative use of flint to form patterns, monograms, inscriptions etc.

GOTHIC English architectural term covering 1200 to 1539, and including EARLY ENGLISH, DECORATED and PERPENDICULAR styles.

GREEN MAN A foliate face, often with leaves coming from its mouth. Seen on fonts, CORBELS etc.

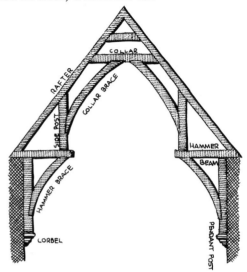

HAMMER BEAM ROOF

HAMMER-BEAMS Beams projecting at right angles, to provide support for vertical members or braces of a wooden roof.

HOOD-MOULD Projecting moulding above an arch or LINTEL to throw off water.

INDENT Matrix for brass.

INDULGENCE See Papal Indulgence.

JESSE (WINDOW) Visual genealogy of Christ's descent from Jesse. Jesse is portrayed at the base of a tree trunk with Christ's other forebears depicted in loops of braches.

LANCET Narrow windows which terminate in a sharp point; characteristic of the EARLY ENGLISH period.

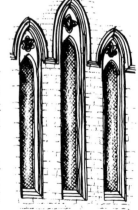

EARLY ENGLISH LANCETS *c.*1220

LECTERN Free standing reading desk.

LEDGER A flat stone covering a grave; often forms part of a church floor.

LINTEL Load-bearing support over door or window.

LONG AND SHORT WORK Alternate vertical and horizontal stonework, used as corner quoins in SAXON churches (*see* drawing for QUOINS).

LOW-SIDE WINDOW A small window low down in the CHANCEL wall, just E of the arch. They were not originally glazed. It is generally thought that a handbell would be rung through the opening at the elevation of the Host during Mass, so that those who heard it could thus share in the Celebration. Their exact purpose is not known for certain.

LUCARNE A vertical opening in the tapering surface of a SPIRE, never glazed (*see* drawings for SPIRE).

LYCH-GATE Roofed gate at entrance to churchyard where coffin was traditionally rested.

MASS DIAL A sun dial showing the times of Mass, usually close by porch or entrance. Also referred to as a Scratch Dial.

MINSTER CHURCH The church of a monastery.

MISERICORD Bracket, often richly carved, on the underside of a hinged choir stall seat which when turned up provided the occupant of the seat with a support during a long period of standing.

NAIL-HEAD EARLY ENGLISH ornamentation, consisting of small nail-like pyramids, regularly repeated.

NAVE *See* CHURCH PLAN.

NORMAN Style of architecture, typified by rounded arches and massive

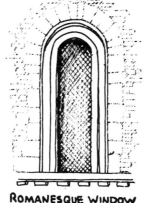

ROMANESQUE WINDOW
c.1150

piers, from 1066 to c.1200. *See also* ROMANESQUE.

OGEE A double curved arch, very characteristic of the DECORATED period.

BLIND OGEE ARCH

PAPAL INDULGENCE Pardon from punishment for sin, granted for an act of devotion.

PARAPET SPIRE *See* SPIRE

PARCLOSE A screen separating a chapel or aisle from the body of the church.

PERPENDICULAR (PERP) Stylistic division of English GOTHIC architecture c.1335-50 to c.1530 (*see* drawing for TRACERY).

PIER A strong solid support, pillar or column.

PISCINA A stone basin, with a drain, for washing the sacred vessels, usually to the S of an altar.

POPPY-HEAD The carved ornament on top of bench-ends or pew-ends.

QUATREFOIL Four-lobed decorative opening or window.

QUOINS Stones at the angles or corners of a building.

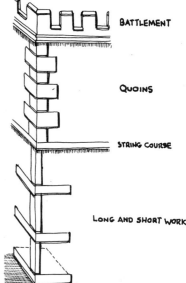

BATTLEMENT

QUOINS

STRING COURSE

LONG AND SHORT WORK

REBUS Pun, representing a name or word by the use of symbol, e.g. Bishop Alcock, represented by a cockerel.

REREDOS Painted or carved screen behind altar.

RETABLE Painted or carved panels behind altar.

ROMANESQUE Architectural style from 9th to 12th centuries. In England known as SAXON and NORMAN. In Britain synonymous with the NORMAN style. On the continent from which it was introduced, the term goes back earlier.

ROOD A cross or crucifix.

ROOD LOFT Gallery on top of ROOD SCREEN, to contain the ROOD and also for use by singers and musicians.

ROOD SCREEN A screen at the entry of the CHANCEL, occasionally in stone, usually in wood; on which was erected the ROOD LOFT or rood beam.

SARSEN STONE Stone traditionally marking meeting place of the Hundred.

SAXON Style of architecture linked with period before Norman Conquest.

SEDILIA Seats for clergy usually on S side of CHANCEL.

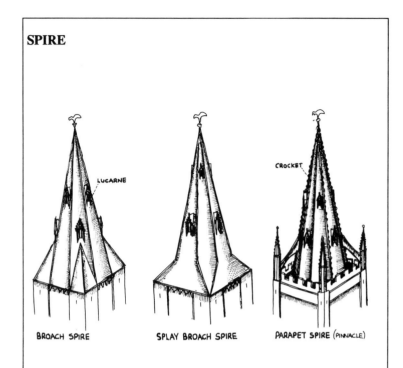

BROACH SPIRE   SPLAY BROACH SPIRE   PARAPET SPIRE (PINNACLE)

BROACH SPIRE Spire rising directly from the tower with no intervening parapet. The corner junctions between the octagon and the square are covered by triangular spurs, or broaches.

PARAPET SPIRE Spire rising behind the parapet, sometimes supported by flying-buttresses. Also called pinnacle spire.

SHEILA-NA-GIG Female (or male) figure displaying genitalia.

SQUINT A hole cut in a wall or through a PIER to allow a view of the main altar of a church.

STEEPLE Tower together with SPIRE, cupola etc.

STIFF LEAF EARLY ENGLISH, 13th century, type of foliage.

STOUP Vessel for the holy water, usually placed by a door.

TRACERY Open pattern of stonework in upper part of GOTHIC windows. Also, can be of wood in screens, etc. or on a solid background to be blind.

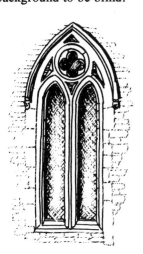

EARLY ENGLISH c. 1240

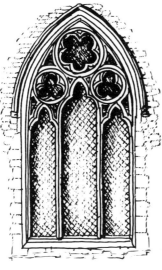

LATE C13 TRANSITIONAL

DECORATED TRACERY

PERPENDICULAR TRACERY

STRING-COURSE A projecting horizontal band set in the surface of a wall. It acts as a division (*see* drawing for QUOINS).

TRANSEPT An arm of a cross-shaped church.

CHEVRON

CAPITAL

ROMANESQUE TYMPANUM

TYMPANUM Area between lintel and arch of a doorway, often filled with a relief sculpture.

VESTRY See CHURCH PLAN

BIBLIOGRAPHY

ANDERSON, M.D., *Looking for History in British Churches* (John Murray, London, 1951)

BETJEMAN, Sir John (ed.), *Parish Churches of England & Wales* (Collins, London, 1980)

BIGMORE, Peter, *The Bedfordshire and Huntingdonshire Landscape* (Hodder and Stoughton, London, 1979)

CLIFTON-TAYLOR, Alec, *English Parish Churches as Works of Art* (B.T. Batsford, London, 1986)

COCKE, T; FINDLAY, D; HALSEY, R; WILLIAMSON, E., *Recording a Church: an illustrated glossary* (Council for British Archaeology, London, 1982)

CONYBEARE E., *Highways & Byways in Cambridge and Ely* (MacMillan and Co., London, 1923)

COOK, G.H., *English Medieval Parish Churches* (Phoenix House, London, 1954)

COWEN, Painton, *A Guide to Stained Glass in Britain* (Michael Joseph, London, 1985)

COX, J. Charles, *Pulpits, Lecterns & Organs* (Oxford University Press, 1915)

HALL, James, *Dictionary of Subjects and Symbols in Art* (John Murray, London, 1987)

MEE, Arthur, *The King's England Cambridgeshire* (Hodder & Stoughton, London, 1965)

MEE, Arthur, *The King's England, Bedfordshire & Huntingdonshire* (Hodder & Stoughton, London, 1973)

MESSENT, Claude J.W. Messent, *Lych-gates and their Churches in Eastern England* (The Author, Blofield, 1970)

PEVSNER, Nikolaus, *Bedfordshire, & the County of Huntingdon and Peterborough* (Penguin Books, Harmondsworth, 1968)

PEVSNER, Nikolaus, *Cambridgeshire* (Penguin Books, Harmondsworth, 1986)

PRITCHARD, V., *English Medieval Graffiti* (Cambridge University Press, Cambridge, 1967)

RAVENSDALE, Jack, *The Domesday Inheritance* (Souvenir Press, London, 1986)

R.C.H.M. *North-East Cambridgeshire* (H.M. Stationery Office, London 1972)

R.C.H.M. *West Cambridgeshire* (H.M. Stationery Office, London, 1968)

RUSSELL, Ronald, *Cambridgeshire and Cambridge* (Shire Publications, Aylesbury, 1988)

SCARFE, Norman, *Cambridgeshire, A Shell Guide*, (Faber & Faber, London, 1983)

TAYLOR, H.M. & J., *Anglo-Saxon Architecture, Vols. I & II* (Cambridge University Press, Cambridge, 1965)

TAYLOR, H.M., *Anglo-Saxon Architecture, Vol.III* (Cambridge University Press, Cambridge, 1978)